Practise it! SMA!

READING & WRITING
for FIRST (FCE)

**Helen Chilton
& Lynda Edwards**

■ SCHOLASTIC

CONTENTS

Practise it! SMASH it!

is an integrated skills series designed to help you prepare for the Cambridge English exams.

This book focuses on Reading and Writing skills in the *Cambridge English: First* and *First for Schools* exams. Each unit gives detailed advice on how to approach different challenges in the tests. They contain a variety of activities to help build and develop your exam skills and there are useful tips on exam technique throughout.

THE READING AND USE OF ENGLISH TEST

In the *Cambridge English: First* Reading and Use of English test you are required to have a wide-ranging vocabulary, as well as knowledge of useful reading techniques.

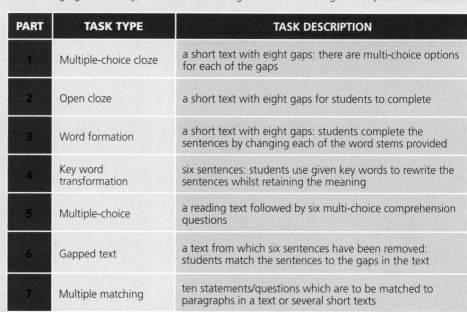

PART	TASK TYPE	TASK DESCRIPTION
1	Multiple-choice cloze	a short text with eight gaps: there are multi-choice options for each of the gaps
2	Open cloze	a short text with eight gaps for students to complete
3	Word formation	a short text with eight gaps: students complete the sentences by changing each of the word stems provided
4	Key word transformation	six sentences: students use given key words to rewrite the sentences whilst retaining the meaning
5	Multiple-choice	a reading text followed by six multi-choice comprehension questions
6	Gapped text	a text from which six sentences have been removed: students match the sentences to the gaps in the text
7	Multiple matching	ten statements/questions which are to be matched to paragraphs in a text or several short texts

Candidates have 75 minutes to do the Reading and Use of English test.

Parts 1–4 contain tasks with a grammar and vocabulary focus.

Parts 5–7 contain a range of texts with accompanying reading comprehension tasks.

THE WRITING TEST

In the *Cambridge English: First* Writing test you need to be able to show clear organisation of ideas, approriate register and style and a good understanding of what each task type requires.

PART	TASK TYPE	TASK DESCRIPTION
1	Discursive essay	You are asked to write a discursive essay in a neutral or formal style. You are given a question or statement and are then asked to give your views on it.
2	Article, email or letter, review, report	You can choose from three different task types. Your writing style should be appropriate to the task type.
2 (For Schools)	Article, email or letter, review, report, story, set text	You can choose from four different task types. Your writing style should reflect the task type. The For Schools exam includes two addittional task types.

Candidates have 80 minutes to do the Writing test.

Part 1 is a compulsory discursive essay.

In Part 2, candidates can choose from three (or four) different task types. Candidates are asked to write between 140 and 190 words for each task.

What's inside?

This book contains **12 units** as well as a complete practice test for each skill. The lessons can be used in any order, depending on the areas you would like to concentrate on.

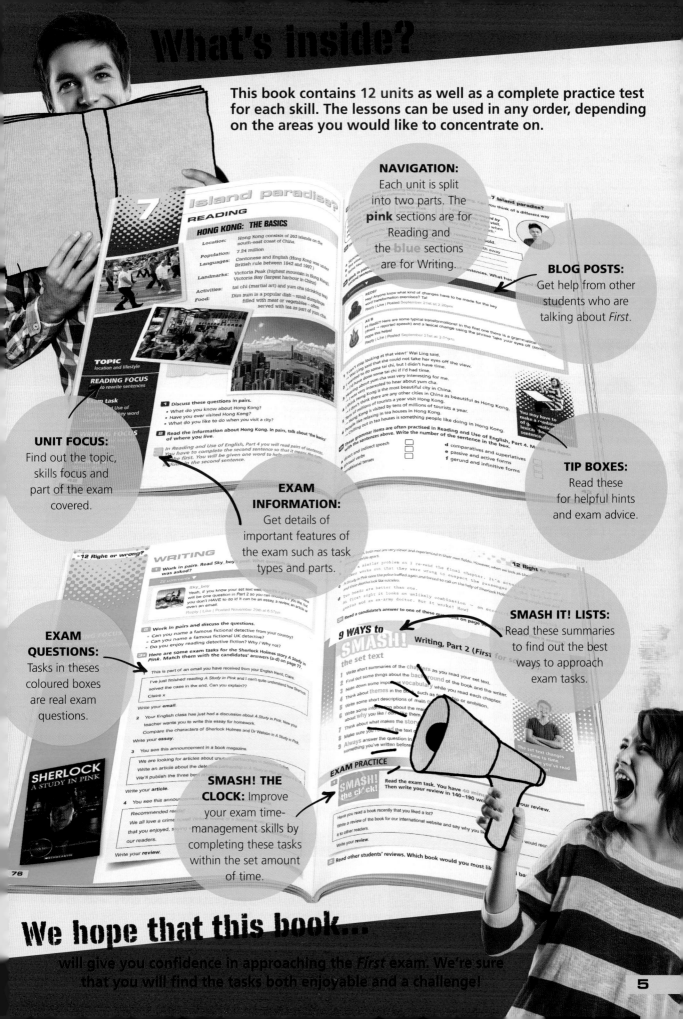

NAVIGATION:
Each unit is split into two parts. The **pink** sections are for Reading and the **blue** sections are for Writing.

BLOG POSTS:
Get help from other students who are talking about *First*.

TIP BOXES:
Read these for helpful hints and exam advice.

UNIT FOCUS:
Find out the topic, skills focus and part of the exam covered.

EXAM INFORMATION:
Get details of important features of the exam such as task types and parts.

SMASH IT! LISTS:
Read these summaries to find out the best ways to approach exam tasks.

EXAM QUESTIONS:
Tasks in theses coloured boxes are real exam questions.

SMASH! THE CLOCK: Improve your exam time-management skills by completing these tasks within the set amount of time.

We hope that this book...

will give you confidence in approaching the *First* exam. We're sure that you will find the tasks both enjoyable and a challenge!

READING

TOPIC
lifestyle

READING FOCUS
how to approach reading texts; reading techniques

Exam task
Reading and Use of English, Parts 5–7

WRITING FOCUS
how to approach the essay question

Exam task
Writing, Part 1

1 Look at the pictures. Discuss these questions in pairs.

- What do you think these people might wish to achieve?
- What would you like to achieve in the near future?
- What would help you achieve this ambition?

The Reading and Use of English test includes different types of texts. These may be a mixture of fiction and non-fiction.

2a Look at the text types in the box. Decide whether each is fiction or non-fiction.

> a news article | a diary | a professional journal | a job advert | a book review | a brochure | a reference book | a novel | an autobiography | a magazine article

2b How often do you read each text type in your everyday life?

3 Read Mac's post. What advice would you give him?

18 comments ▼

Mac
Hey, everyone! I'm taking the First exam soon and I never do very well in the Reading test. Any ideas how to improve my reading skills in English? Cheers, Mac.

Reply | Like | Posted April 21st at 3.00pm

4 Look at these ways of improving reading skills in English. Tick the things you already do. Which would you consider trying?

- Read articles which are written at a level slightly above your current level of English.
- Read the title of an article and predict what the article might be about before you read it.
- Ignore any words you don't know – read for the main message of a text.
- Read things in English that you enjoy in your own language, e.g. magazines, comics.
- Practise summarising what a text is about to a friend or member of your family.
- Work with a friend and choose an article that you both enjoy reading. Write questions about the article to test each other's understanding.

5a Predicting, skimming, scanning and reading for detail are all reading techniques you can use in the Reading and Use of English test. Match the techniques (1–4) with their definitions (a–d).

1 predicting		**a** reading very carefully to grasp specific meaning
2 skimming		**b** looking through a text quickly to find particular information
3 scanning		**c** thinking about what information a text might include
4 reading for detail		**d** reading the whole text quickly to get a general impression

5b When would you use each technique? Look at the stages and discuss your ideas in pairs. (More than one technique may be appropriate for each stage.)

a the test instructions
b the title and sub-heading
c finding out what the text is about in general
d the question and options
e finding a name, number or other word / phrase
f locating a particular idea in the text
g checking your answer is correct

Answer every question. If there are any you aren't sure about, go back and check them at the end.

6 Work in pairs. Read the *Smash It!* list. Which of the techniques will you try to use?

6 WAYS to

SMASH!

Reading & Use of English, Parts 5–7:

reading techniques

1 Read the **instructions** carefully to find out what you have to do. It may include information about the **content** of the text.

2 Read the **title** and any **sub-headings** and consider what the text might be about. Don't spend long on this!

3 Read the whole text quickly to give you an idea of the **overall message**.

4 Read each **question** and the answer options carefully.

5 Locate the **section** where each question is answered in the text.

6 Read the relevant section of the text **in detail** and choose or write your **answer**.

1a Read the instructions for a Reading and Use of English, Part 5 task. What kind of text are you going to read? What is it about? What do you have to do?

You are going to read a magazine article about achieving goals. For questions 1–6, choose the answer (A, B, C or D) which you think fits best according to the text.

1b Read the title of the article and the text in italics. What additional information have you found out? What kind of information do you think will be included in the text?

2a Read the article and answer these questions.
a What is Jade's ambition?   b Who is going to help her achieve it?   c Who is her favourite sportsperson?

Extreme goal makeover!

Our professional life coach helped one teen turn her big dream into an achievable action plan. Read how they did it.

Of course you want this school year to be A+ and awesome. But it won't happen unless you make it happen! To prove that achieving your goals is totally doable, we've taken a teen and her dream and paired her with a coach who fine-tuned her objectives and action plan. The result: a new path to success that seems clear, not overwhelming. So steal their secrets – then go for it!

Jade Raynor wants to represent her country as a professional swimmer. As a naturally competitive high school student, Jade's always worked hard, but now she's at a crossroads and will really have to focus if she wants to be a pro swimmer.

'If Jade wants to represent her country in swimming, she'll have to get serious,' says her life coach Ailish Campbell. 'One way in which she can do this is to focus on one or two swimming strokes and devote her time and effort to getting them right. With the help of her trainer, Jade should design a one-hour strength-training regime tailored to these strokes, which she'll put into practice twice a week.'

Jade also needs to be more consistent in her eating and sleeping habits by getting 8–9 hours of rest per night and consuming lots of lean protein and carbs at every meal. In addition, Jade has to work on building a winning mindset. Her favourite Olympian of all time is Missy Franklin; Missy reminds Jade that anything is possible. So Jade could find photographs of Missy winning gold and put them up in her sports locker and bedroom to help her visualise success.

2b Now answer this multiple-choice question.

What does Ailish Campbell think Jade needs to do?

A ask her coach to show her some new techniques

B focus more on swimming than schoolwork

C increase the number of practice sessions

D re-think her approach to training

WRITING

1a Work in pairs. Read Lydia's post. What do you know about the essay question?

5 comments ▼

Lydia
First Writing has always got an essay question, is that right? I'm not sure what this is like. Can anyone point me in the right direction?
Reply | Like | Posted April 30th at 2.10pm

1b Read the Q&A page that Big_ears recommends to check your ideas.

6 comments ▼

Big_ears
I found this Q & A page about the essay really helpful!
Reply | Like | Posted April 30th at 2.25pm

WRITING FOCUS
how to approach the
essay question
Exam task
Writing, Part 1

Part 1: the Essay

Q: Do we HAVE to do the essay question, or is there a choice?

A: The essay question is compulsory.

Q: How is the essay question usually phrased?

A: There are 3 parts!

- a set-up, e.g. *In your class you've been talking about money.*
- an essay question, e.g. *Is it better to save money or spend it?*
- three points to include: two are given to you and one you need to come up with, e.g.
  1 enjoyment   2 security   3 (your own idea)

Q: If we have to write about three points, together with an introduction and a conclusion, then that makes five paragraphs, is that right?

A: It's true that there should be an introduction and a conclusion but sometimes you can combine two points into one paragraph.

Q: Is there a right or wrong answer to the essay question?

A: No, just your own ideas and opinions.

Q: If we don't write about all the points, do we lose marks?

A: Yes, sorry! You have to include all the information the question asks for.

Q: Is it important to keep to the word limit?

A: Try to stay as close to the limit – between 140 and 190 words – as you can. A little longer or shorter isn't going to be a problem. But if you write TOO little, you probably haven't covered everything. And if you write TOO much you've probably included some irrelevant points!

2 Work in pairs. Do you know these people? What skills did they need to get where they are? Who would you prefer to be? Why?

3a Read the essay question. In your pairs, discuss what you could say about points 1 and 2, and then think of some ideas for point 3.

In your English class you have been talking about high achievers and the consequences of success. Now, your English teacher has asked you to write an essay.

Write an essay using **all** the notes and giving reasons for your point of view.

Is staying at the top more difficult than reaching it?

Notes

Write about:

1. people's expectations

2. motivation

3. .... (your own idea)

3b Read a candidate's answer on page 94 and compare your ideas.

4 Read the essay on page 94 again. Find and underline the following:

    a a statement to introduce the topic
    b a phrase that is used to sum up in the conclusion
    c examples of a range of different grammatical structures

8 WAYS to SMASH! the essay

Writing, Part 1:

1. Read the question carefully and include all the points in your answer.
2. Divide your essay into several paragraphs that follow logically.
3. Always give a brief introduction and conclusion.
4. Stay on the topic and don't write about irrelevant things.
5. Give examples, where appropriate, to clarify your points.
6. Make a plan and note down points for each paragraph before you write.
7. Use a variety of structures and vocabulary.
8. Always read through your essay afterwards and check your grammar, spelling and punctuation.

EXAM PRACTICE

1a Read the two exam tasks and discuss what you could include for the third point each time.

In your English class you have been talking about becoming famous. Now, your English teacher has asked you to write an essay.

Write an essay using **all** the notes and giving reasons for your point of view.

Fame can bring more problems than benefits. Do you agree?

Notes

Write about:

1. lifestyle

2. privacy

3. .... (your own idea)

In your English class you have been talking about celebrity. Now, your English teacher has asked you to write an essay.

Write an essay using all the notes and giving reasons for your point of view.

Anyone can become famous if they really want to and work hard. Do you agree?

Notes

Write about:

1. talent

2. opportunity

3. .... (your own idea)

1b Read the *Smash It!* list above. Then choose one of the tasks and write your essay in 140–190 words.

2 Binge-watching

READING

TOPIC
entertainment

READING FOCUS
how to understand the instructions
Exam task
Reading and Use of English, Parts 1–7

WRITING FOCUS
how to approach the story task
Exam task
Writing, Part 2 (*First for Schools*): story

1 Look at the pictures of characters from popular sitcoms. Discuss these questions in pairs.

- Do you know which sitcoms the characters are from?
- Why do you think people watch sitcoms? Do you find them funny?
- How realistic do you think sitcom characters are?
- Do you ever 'binge watch' your favourite sitcoms? ('Binge-watching' means watching lots of episodes one after another.)

The Reading and Use of English test has different task types, which include multiple choice, gap fill, multiple matching and transformations.

2a Look at the extracts on page 13 from Parts 1–4 of the *First* Reading and Use of English test. Which is the task in each case? Choose from the following:

- writing the correct form of a word to fill a gap
- completing a text with a missing sentence
- answering a multiple-choice question
- matching a text and question
- writing a missing word
- re-writing part of a sentence

and box sets

Part 1   Read the text below and decide which answer (**A**, **B**, **C** or **D**) best fits the gap.

Sitcoms are TV shows in which a group of characters are .... in amusing situations.

A affected   **B** involved   **C** arranged   **D** concerned

Part 2   Read the text below and think of the word which best fits the gap.

One .... the most popular American sitcoms is *The Big Bang Theory* which was first broadcast in 2007.

Part 3   Read the text below. Use the word given in capitals at the end of the line to form a word that fits in the gap.

Over the last twenty or so years, *Friends* has been watched by millions, and **(1)** .... became   **VIEW**

hooked on the lives of the a television series in which the same characters are involved in amusing

situations in each show.

Part 4   Complete the second sentence so that it has a similar meaning to the first sentence, using the word given.
Do not change the word given.

20-somethings enjoyed watching the show because it was about people like themselves.

The show .... enjoyed it because it was about people like themselves.   **WHO**

2b Now complete the tasks.

3a Read the instructions for Parts 5–7 of the *First* Reading and Use of English test. Underline the key words in the instructions which will help you do the task.

Part 5   You are going to read an article about what makes a sitcom successful. For questions **31 – 36**, choose the answer (**A**, **B**, **C** or **D**) which you think fits best according to the text.

Part 6   You are going to read a magazine article about humour in sitcoms. Six sentences have been removed from the article. Choose from the sentences **A – G** the one which fits each gap (**37 – 42**).

Part 7   You are going to read a newspaper article about a sitcom actor. For questions **43 – 52**, choose from the sections (**A – D**). The sections may be chosen more than once.

3b For Parts 5–7, which is the task in each case? Choose from the list on page 12.

3c Look at the task instructions for Parts 5–7 again. Answer these questions.
  a In which task will you find out about what makes people laugh when watching sitcoms?
  b In which task will you discover the secrets of making a really good sitcom?
  c In which task will you learn about someone who works on a sitcom?

5 WAYS to SMASH!

Reading & Use of English:

understanding the instructions

1 Read the instructions **before** you start reading the questions and texts. Pay careful attention to the instructions in **bold**.

2 <u>Underline</u> key words in the instructions which might help you to complete the task.

3 Look back at the instructions during the test to **make sure** you're doing the right thing.

4 Parts 1–4 of the Reading and Use of English test provide an **example** of what to do. Read these before you start writing your **answers**.

5 Parts 5–7 of the Reading and Use of English test require you to read **longer texts**. The instructions will give you an idea of what you're going to read about.

EXAM PRACTICE

1a **In pairs, look at these shortened exam tasks. Discuss what you have to do for each task.**

Part 6

The Big Bang Theory is about a group of four geeky friends. It tells the story of Leonard and Sheldon, who share a flat, and their friends Howard and Raj. Leonard has a neighbour named Penny, who he fancies. Unlike *Friends*, *The Big Bang Theory* has a lot of jokes about geek culture, such as *Star Wars* and *Star Trek*. Many people would agree that *The Big Bang Theory* is the best show on television. **1** [ ] They also love to laugh at Sheldon's hilarious social faux pas. The show has helped make 'geek' cool, changing the meaning of the word in the English language.

A The greatest number of people watching the show since it first came onto our screens was 20.44 million.

B They switch on once a week to watch the adorable relationship between Leonard and Penny and to see Raj getting rejected by yet another woman.

C Its target audience is people aged between 18 and 49.

Part 7

Which character in the show

was considered unusual? **1** [ ]

enjoyed looking after her friends? **2** [ ]

didn't seem capable of doing anything useful at first? **3** [ ]

A Rachel started out as a spoiled rich kid, who was naïve but also determined and brave and who eventually became a successful businesswoman in her own right.

B Monica, the 'mother hen' of the group of friends, was known for her obsessive cleanliness and desire to compete with others.

C The 'ditzy' one of the group, Phoebe had an innocent, childlike personality, and is arguably the show's most eccentric character.

> **Most of the texts have a title – don't ignore this as it may help you understand the text!**

1b Now complete the tasks.

WRITING

1 Read A1ko's post. What advice can you give her?

11 comments ▼

 A1ko I'm really not sure how to approach the story task in the First for Schools exam. What sort of questions do they give you? What if I don't have any ideas?
Reply | Like | Posted May 7th 5.12pm

2a Read the story task. What do you need to incorporate into your story?

You have seen this notice in an international students' magazine.

> **Send us your stories**
>
> We're looking for some stories to publish in the fiction section of our magazine.
>
> The story must begin with the sentence:
>
> *It was the day of my audition and I was feeling very nervous.*
>
> Your story must include:
>
> * a song
> * some water

2b Work in pairs and answer these questions to help you come up with a story.

a What was the audition for?
b Why had you decided to do it?
c Why were you feeling nervous?
d Where were you at the beginning of the story?
e Did anything unusual happen?
f Who sang the song?
g Where was the water? Where did it come from?
h What happened at the end?

3 Read the sample story on page 16 and answer these questions.

a Which of the questions from exercise 2 did the writer answer?
b Is the story well-organised?
c What effect does the dialogue have on the story?

4 Find adjectives in the story which mean the same as each of these words.

a very loud   **b** very scared (x2)
c very good (x3)   **d** very quiet

Read the opening sentence and the points to include, then ask yourself some questions to get some ideas.

WRITING FOCUS
how to approach the story task

Exam task
Writing, Part 2 (*First for Schools*): story

SAMPLE STORY Audition day

It was the day of my audition and I was feeling very nervous. My sister had applied for me to audition for a TV talent show without asking me! I love dancing but I HATE performing in front of lots of people! I was standing there at the side of the stage and feeling terrified.

The young guy before me was brilliant. He had a wonderful voice and he was singing one of my favourite songs. When he finished, everyone stood up and applauded, including the judges. 'Don't worry,' he said to me as he passed. 'The audience is great.'

'Sure,' I thought. 'Great for you!'

Tentatively I stepped out into the spotlight. I started my dance and everything was going well until suddenly my foot slipped on some water. I crashed to the floor. Everyone in the room was completely silent. I stood up shakily. Should I leave? Then I saw one of the judges. He was smiling and he gave me a 'thumbs up'.

So I finished my dance and the roar from the audience was deafening. I was going to be in the finals on television!

5 Work in pairs and think of strong adjectives to replace those below.

a very tired ....*exhausted*.....   f very big ....
b very angry ....   g very crowded ....
c very happy ....   h very small ....
d very cold ....   i very dirty ....
e very bad ....   j very funny ....

REMEMBER!
We cannot use 'very' with these strong adjectives.

very tired ✓
exhausted ✓
very exhausted ✗

6 Work in pairs. Can you add sentences to the story using the adjectives above? The sentences could be about events before the story begins, during the story or afterwards.

Example: *The writer was furious when she found out what her sister had done.*

6 WAYS to SMASH!

Writing, Part 2 (*First for Schools*):

approaching the story task

1 Read the question carefully, especially the sentence you need to use and the things to include.

2 Get some ideas by asking yourself questions about the situation.

Where is the person? How does he feel? What could the items be used for?

3 Other sources of inspiration could come from things that have happened to you or someone you know – or even something you've read about.

4 Divide your story into clear paragraphs. Start by setting the scene, follow with paragraphs that describe the different events, and finish with an interesting, funny or dramatic ending.

5 Adding some dialogue to your story can make it come alive.

6 Make your story exciting by using strong adjectives, e.g. *furious, hilarious, terrifying*.

1 **Discuss these questions in pairs.**

- What can you see in the pictures?
- How do you think the performers are feeling?
- Would you like to enter a talent competition? Why / Why not?
- What sort of things can go wrong in a performance?

2 **Read the exam task. In pairs, think of two things to include in the story. Swap your task with another pair. Now write this story in 140–190 words.**

You have seen this notice in an international students' magazine.

> **Send us your stories!**
>
> We're looking for some stories to publish in the fiction section of our magazine. The story must begin with
>
> the sentence:
>
> *The performance had been going so well but then things started to go wrong.*
>
> Your story must include:
>
> - ....
> - ....

Write your **story**.

3 **Share your stories with the rest of the class. Whose is the most unusual?**

3

Looking good?

TOPIC
image and fashion

READING FOCUS
how to deal with unfamiliar vocabulary

Exam task
Reading and Use of English, Part 5: multiple choice

WRITING FOCUS
how to use informal and more formal language in emails

Exam task
Writing, Part 2: email

READING

1 Discuss these questions in pairs.

- Do you spend a lot of time doing exercise to get fit? Why? / Why not?
- Do you think some people do too much exercise? Why? / Why not?
- Apart from exercise, what else is important for a healthy lifestyle?

2 Read the post. What tips would you give Goggles? Discuss in pairs.

9 comments ▼

Goggles
I need some advice here. What if I can't answer the reading questions because I don't know some of the words?
Reply | Like | Posted May 14th at 6.21pm

3 Look at the title and introduction for this magazine article. Work in pairs and answer the questions.

- What do you think the article will be about?
- What do you think are the meanings of 'quick fix' and 'hooked on'? How do you know this?

THE QUICK FIX:
Solution or problem?

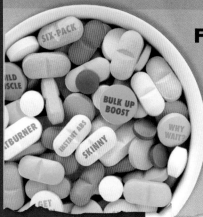

From fast-action protein drinks to instant diet pills – are young people hooked on 'quick fixes' to change their looks?

4 Read the first part of the article and answer the questions.

'When I was at college, I was pretty average-looking and had a lot of 'puppy fat',' says Luke. 'I felt quite **self-conscious** about it.' So Luke headed to the gym to **bulk up** and burn off fat. But soon he became discouraged. 'I really wanted to have a **six-pack** and it wasn't happening fast enough. A couple of guys I knew told me about **protein shakes**. They were taking them and they looked great.'

Like many people, Luke was **seeking** a quick fix – in this case, to transform his **physique**. And why not you might ask. 'It's **human nature** to look for the quickest, easiest way to get what we want,' says the Essential Life Skills website. 'We want to find the product or programme that will fix us and make everything all right and we want it overnight!'

Starting with two protein shakes a day, Luke **built up to** seven shakes daily, using the shakes to replace meals. But his improved appearance **came at a price**. He experienced trembling **limbs** and bursts of sudden anger. 'I'd get angry at the smallest things,' says Luke. 'I even split up with my girlfriend, Zoe.' This raises the question: are quick fixes really a solution – or a problem?

When you first read through the text, ignore any new or difficult words. Sometimes you can answer the questions without knowing them!

a Complete the summary sentence for this section of the article.

Luke wanted to ....

because ....

but ....

b What is the writer's attitude?

   A It's understandable for people to try a quick fix.

   B It's very dangerous to take protein shakes.

   C It's important to try to look good.

c Did you need to understand all the words in the article to answer these questions?

5 Look at the words in bold in the article. Use the clues to write a synonym / definition for each word.

a self-conscious

....

> Look at the previous sentence. How does Luke feel?

b bulk up

....

> This is a verb + preposition 'up' which sometimes suggests 'more' (e.g. *turn up the volume*). Why do people often go to the gym?

c six-pack

....

> Think about the number 6 – what could it refer to? When do we use the word 'pack'?

d protein shakes

....

> Luke starts taking these. Read paragraph 3 to find the meaning.

e seeking

....

> Think of another verb that could be used with 'a quick fix' in this context.

f physique

....

> Think of other words you know beginning with 'phys-'. What did Luke want to change about himself?

g human nature

....

> Think about the individual meaning of both words.

h built up to

....

> Compare the first and second parts of the sentence. What changed?

i came at a price

....

> Look at the next sentence – it gives an example. Note that 'price' does not only refer to money.

j limbs

....

> Read the whole sentence. Luke is experiencing physical and emotional reactions. Which parts of our body can tremble?

6 WAYS to SMASH!

Reading & Use of English, Part 5:

unfamiliar vocabulary

1 Look at the previous sentence to see if the word links back to something there.

> Doing exercise can be like a drug. If you don't do much
> for a while you get a **craving** for it!

2 Look at the next sentence to see if it is explained or if there is an example.

> He's **lost** a lot of **weight**. When I saw him, he was really thin.

3 Look at the part of speech and whether it's singular or plural. Does it have a root that you recognise?

> Kyle got really **argumentative**.

4 See if you recognise any parts of the word, or individual words in a compound, phrase or collocation that might help you.

> He was also getting **bad mood swings**.

5 Look at the rest of the text to see if the word reappears or is rephrased.

6 Be sensible! Check that the meaning you guess makes sense with the rest of the sentence and context.

EXAM PRACTICE

In Reading and Use of English, Part 5 there is always a multiple-choice question about the meaning of a difficult word or phrase.

1 Read the rest of the article on page 21 and choose the best answers.

1 The writer uses the phrase 'promising a shortcut' in line 6 to indicate that the producers believe …

  A their product is the best.

  B their product is a quick means of achieving a goal.

  C the results of using their product will be long-lasting.

  D the users of their product will be admired by everyone.

2 What does the phrase 'there's an elephant in the room' in line 19 refer to?

  A something that people have forgotten about

  B too much concern about size and appearance

  C something obvious that people don't want to talk about

  D something dangerous that people aren't aware of

3 'Reputable brands' in line 40 are products …

  A that aren't easily available.

  B that are bought because of personal recommendations.

  C that are effective and therefore expensive.

  D that are well-known and proven to be dependable.

4 What does the phrase 'proverbial band aid' mean?

  A an old fashioned remedy that used to work

  B advice with an element of truth

  C a temporary measure to treat a wound

  D an achievable goal

THE QUICK FIX:
Solution or problem?

Take Luke's protein shakes, for instance. 'Classic protein drinks as well as powders and bars target hard-core gym-goers and athletes,' says the BBC. 5 Their labels often depict six-packs and massive biceps, promising a shortcut to a bulging muscular body.

No wonder the 'sport-related' protein product sector is booming. Within 10 three years it's estimated that the world will consume protein drinks, bars and other supplements worth £8 billion (€10 billion) a year. There's even a new wave of protein products 15 in the UK – dairy drinks like For

Goodness Shakes and Upbeat – aimed merely at so-called 'healthy lifestyle' seekers.

'But there's an elephant in the room,' 20 says the BBC. 'We can't just ignore this.' While protein is essential in the diet for healthy body tissues, muscle and bone mass, we know that most people in the West already eat more 25 than enough protein and adding protein supplements can harm your body – especially the kidneys. 'I got really bad stomach cramps,' Luke says. 'The doctor told me I could do serious 30 damage to my kidneys if I carried on like that.'

'Worse', says Australia's Sydney Morning Herald, 'teens are buying unregulated protein products, particularly powders, 35 over the Internet – often made with dangerous mystery ingredients.' The Herald goes on to say, 'Experts are urging body-conscious teenage boys, gym junkies and people trying to lose 40 weight to buy only reputable brands and check all labels carefully.'

Enter the latest diet craze: raspberry ketones. These have been touted as the next weight-loss miracle drug, 45 with manufacturers claiming that they help your body break down fat more efficiently. But they have never been tested on humans in any scientific study to prove that they are either 50 efficient or safe. What is certain is that high levels in the blood are toxic. 'Once again,' says The Mirror, 'of the vast array of legal and illegal diet pills and supplements available online or in 55 the shops, many are simply ineffectual. But others are potentially fatal.'

'Most of us don't want to hear this but there are no quick fixes or shortcuts to personal appearance, development 60 or anything else worthwhile for that matter,' says the Essential Life Skills website. 'A quick fix for any problem is only meant to hold things together until an effective long-term solution 65 is found. It's merely the proverbial band-aid.'

March issue | 167

2 Work in pairs. Choose three unfamiliar words from the text above or on page 19. Check the meaning and write some multiple-choice questions like those in exercise 1 on page 20. Swap questions with another pair.

3 Discuss these questions in pairs.

- Were you or someone you used to know self-conscious about anything when you were younger?
- Do you think it's a good thing for every guy to want a six-pack?
- Whose physique do you most admire?
- Are you hooked on any particular foods or drinks?
- Have you recently been in a situation where there was 'an elephant in the room'?
- Are shortcuts always a bad idea? Why / Why not?
- Are there occasions when you would buy a product from a brand that was NOT reputable? Why?

GET CHATTY!
If you want to remember new vocabulary, it's important to use the words really soon. Why don't you speak to a friend in English? Try to use the words in the next twenty-four hours!

WRITING

11 comments ▼

Danny

Hi everyone! I've got (another!!!) writing task to do. What do I need to know about writing formal and informal emails? I know you guys can help me! ☺

Reply | Like | Posted March 2nd at 1.30pm

WRITING FOCUS
how to use informal and more formal language in emails

Exam task
Writing, Part 2: email

1 **Read Danny's post. Do you use different language when you're writing emails to friends rather than strangers? List three things that change depending on the recipient. Work in pairs.**

2 **Read the email and answer the questions.**

  a Why is Beth writing the email?
  b Does she know the person she is writing to?
  c Why has the teacher underlined the words and phrases?
  d Can you rephrase these in a more appropriate way?

Hello Sir,

How are you? I'm writing to ask for some information about the fashion design course next year. At the moment I'm studying fashion at school. I love it! It's a really cool subject! So I've got a couple of questions.

First up, how long is it? Secondly, is it expensive? My parents aren't too keen on spending a LOT of money ...

I guess the next thing that happens is you send me a form to fill in. Any chance you could send it this week? Thanks. I'd really love to go to your college as it's got a great reputation and the teachers are really good.

Write soon. ☺ Beth Banks

---

3 **Add examples to the table from the word box.**

	Informal emails	More formal emails
1	Hi Paul, ……...............	Dear Sir / Madam, ……...............
2	………………………………………………	I am writing to request …
3	Take care. ……...............	Regards, ……............... , ……...............
4	Contractions: I'm, they're, ……............... , ……...............	No contractions: I am, ……............... , ……............... , ……...............
5	Incomplete / short sentences: How cool is that! , ……............... I was totally amazed!	Complete sentences: That sounds a very good idea. ……………………………………………… .
6	Chatty language: so, ……...............	More formal equivalents: ……............... , consequently
7	Exclamation marks and dot, dot, dot are OK …!!	No exclamation marks or dot dot dot.

I was very surprised to hear your news. | because of this | Dear Mr Browne | Hello Amy | They are | Love, J |
I thought I'd drop you a line to say … | it's | Sounds great! | therefore |
Yours faithfully | it is | Yours sincerely | I would | I'd

4 Read the email and online job advert and underline examples of informal and more formal language.

A: Email

Hi Eva,

How's it going? I'm doing some research for my fashion blog about global trends and I need your help! It would be great if you could tell me what's trending in Germany at the moment. Which looks are hot right now and who's cool? 😜 Have you or any of your mates got Pinterest pages?

Love

Charlie x

B: Online job advertisement

★ *Hipster Central* ★

An exciting vacancy has arisen at **Hipster Central** magazine for an online fashion blogger. The successful candidate will research and write a weekly blog for our website. Our target market is young adults and we are looking for someone who is both interested in fashion and can relate directly to our readers. If you are creative and fashion-conscious with a background in journalism, please contact alicepearce@newlookmag.com explaining why you feel you would be suitable for the position.

5 Read the response to the job advertisement on page 94. Work in pairs and find examples of phrases that show the formality of the language.

EXAM PRACTICE

1 Discuss these questions in pairs.

* Are you influenced by trends and celebrity fashion?
* What qualities do you need to work in the fashion business?

2 Write an email in answer to Charlie's email above, using an appropriate style. Follow these steps:

1 Note down your ideas and group these into different paragraphs.
2 Write a first draft and then check it.
3 Write your final email in 140–190 words.

3 Exchange emails with your partner. Did you write about similar things? Is the letter written in an appropriate style?

REMEMBER TO THINK ABOUT:
* greetings and endings
* colloquialisms
* contractions
* short or long sentences
* choice of vocabulary
* standard starting and closing sentences

READING

1 Look at the pictures. Discuss these questions in pairs.

- How do you think the people feel? Why?
- What pressure are they under?
- How do you think they should handle each situation?
- How do you deal with pressure? Are you cool and calm, or anxious and irritated?
- What kinds of things make you feel stressed in your daily life?

2 Complete the phrases in bold with the verbs in the box.

burst | get | keep | lose

a I tend to .... **my temper** when things go wrong. I can shout pretty loudly!

b Sara can .... **a bit down** when she gets stressed – she seems really fed up sometimes!

c You seem to .... **cool** under pressure!

d I often .... **into tears** when something's worrying me.

3 Read Sara88's post. Then look at some types of phrase you might find in Reading and Use of English, Part 1. Match them with the definitions.

---

6 comments ▼

Sara88

Hi, I'm trying to learn some phrases to help me with Reading and Use of English, Part 1. Any ideas what to do? Thanks.

Reply | Like | Posted June 2nd at 3.50pm

---

1 collocations

a These consist of more than one part, usually a verb + adverb / preposition. Often the same verb has a literal and metaphorical meaning, e.g. *Could you take your jacket off? / The new product really took off.*

2 idioms

b These are phrases which have a different meaning from the meanings of the separate words, e.g. *I'm over the moon about getting my new job!* ('Over the moon' means very happy.)

3 phrasal verbs

c These are words which are commonly used together, e.g. *catch + a bus / a train / a plane.*

4 Read the text. Match the types of phrase with the words in bold.

*'As a competitive snowboarder, people often ask me how I **stay calm** and confident when **the heat is on**. The reason I **took up** snowboarding was to have fun, so I talk to friends and listen to music instead of thinking about the contest – and the fear just melts away!'*

Jen Goodman, 15, snowboarder

a a collocation .... **b** an idiom ....

c a phrasal verb ....

5 Read about how other young sportspeople deal with pressure and look at the words in bold. Which word could you use instead? Choose a or b.

Max Aaron, 21, figure skater

'Any time fear **creeps** in, I stop and remember that I know how to do this. I think of all the times I've done this routine in training.'

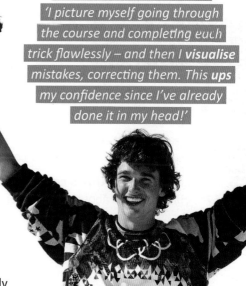

Nick Goepper, 19, freeskier

'I picture myself going through the course and completing each trick flawlessly – and then I **visualise** mistakes, correcting them. This **ups** my confidence since I've already done it in my head!'

1 visualise   **a** imagine   **b** ignore

2 ups   **a** jumps   **b** increases

3 creeps   **a** appears suddenly   **b** enters slowly

6a Read I ❤ BIKE's post and look at the list she is making.

16 comments ▼

I ❤ BIKE

Hi Sara88, It's a good idea to keep a record of phrases on the same topic. At the moment, I'm making a list of some which are used to talk about emotions and being under pressure.

Reply | Like | Posted June 21st at 11.23 am

adjective	phrasal verbs	noun / verb phrase

6b Look at the words and phrases in the box. What part of speech are they? Write them on the list.

anxious | be in a panic | be under stress | calm down | can't relax | chill out | cool | irritated | nervous | stress-free | stress someone out

6c Which words or phrases express positive feelings? Which ones express negative feelings?

5 WAYS to
SMASH!

Reading & Use of English, Part 1:

multiple-choice cloze

1 Read the **whole** text first to gain a general understanding.

2 As you read, **think** about which word might be missing from each gap.

3 Read the text again carefully. Read the words **before** and **after** each gap. The missing word may be part of a phrase, idiom or collocation.

4 Look at the **options** carefully. The words will all have a similar meaning, but only one of them is correct. Think about which option fits grammatically and contextually.

5 Read the whole text again, inserting the options you've chosen to check they sound **right**.

EXAM PRACTICE

In Reading and Use of English, Part 1 you will read a text with gaps to complete. Each gap has four possible options for you to choose from. Only one option is correct.

1  **Cover up questions 1–8 under the text below. Skim the text quickly to find out what the text is about. You have three minutes to complete this task.**

2 Read the *Smash It!* list on page 26. Which of these ways did you use in exercise 1?

3 For questions 1–8, read the text below and decide which answer (A–D) fits best in each gap. There is an example at the beginning.

Example:

0 A certainly   B really   C totally   D literally

0	A	B	C	D
	⎯	▬	⎯	⎯

Pressing pause: think before you act!

'Oh no! Did I (0) .... just send that text?' Most people have said something they immediately wish they could take back – and if they'd paused to think first, they might have acted differently. Pausing doesn't only (1) .... when you speak. Scientific studies have (2) .... that making a habit of pausing before you say or do something can actually have a (3) .... impact on how your life turns out.

By practising pausing – (4) .... a deep breath, counting to ten, or asking yourself 'Is it worth it?' – you can actually change your brain. This means that, over time, pausing becomes your natural (5) .... By making this change, people are more likely to enjoy the life rewards that come with (6) .... levels of self-control – better relationships, higher income, (7) .... promotion. You never know, teaching yourself to pause might just help you (8) .... your life!

1	A pay off	B take over	C get through	D catch up
2	A exposed	B informed	C revealed	D decided
3	A major	B main	C primary	D principal
4	A catching	B making	C doing	D taking
5	A answer	B response	C reply	D prompt
6	A large	B deep	C high	D steep
7	A acquiring	B reaching	C fulfilling	D gaining
8	A boost	B transform	C profit	D reconstruct

Go with your instincts if you aren't sure! Quite often, your first choice is the correct one because you've probably heard the phrase before.

4 Look at the *Smash It!* list again. How many of the ways did you manage to use in exercise 3?

WRITING

1 **Discuss these questions in pairs.**

- How often do you read articles in magazines, newspapers or online?
- What makes an article boring? How can you make an article less boring?

2 **Read these posts and the *Smash It!* list that wise_guy recommends. Which points on the list do you find particularly useful?**

WRITING FOCUS
how to use the correct tone and add interest to an article

Exam task
Writing, Part 2: article

---

4 comments ▼

UNA
Hi, wise_guy! How can I make my articles more interesting? Even I get bored when I read them – not a good sign!
Reply | Like | Posted October 8th at 3.00pm

wise_guy
You've got to get the reader's attention. Smash It! has some great tips on this!
Reply | Like | Posted October 9th at 11.00am

---

8 WAYS to SMASH!

Writing, Part 2:

writing an interesting article

1 Give it a **catchy** title.

2 **Engage** the reader by talking directly to him / her.

3 Use some short sentences to add drama.

4 Use strong adjectives to **emphasise** points.

5 Add some **humour** if you can.

6 Use occasional exclamation marks**!**

7 Use some **idioms** / colloquial language.

8 Give it an **ending** that is amusing or makes us think. This could also be a question to the reader.

3a **Look at the exam task. Read the two articles on page 95. Both articles are well-organised and grammatically correct. One was written *before* and one *after* reading the *Smash It!* list. Which was written after?**

You have seen this advertisement in a magazine.

Decisions! Decisions!

We're looking for articles about big decisions people have made and whether they were right or not! Send us your article and you could win £100 and have your article published in our next issue.

3b **Read the *Smash It!* list again. Find examples of the eight ways in the more interesting article.**

4 In the more interesting article, how does the writer rephrase these ideas in more colloquial language?

a It's easy to talk about something, but it's harder to do it.

b The final responsibility is ours.

c do the right thing

d I wouldn't be good at …

e continue

f stop doing something

g This is an example of …

h do what you feel naturally is right

5 Work in pairs. Think of …

• … something that is easier said than done.

• … something you are not cut out for.

• … something that you should give up.

• … a time when people should follow their instincts.

EXAM PRACTICE

1 Work in pairs. Here are some events in our lives that can prove particularly stressful. Talk about the types of pressure that people can experience at these different times.

2 Read the exam task and follow these steps.

1 Decide what you are going to write about.

2 Plan your article and make notes for the different paragraphs.

3 Think of an interesting title, opening and ending.

4 Write your article in 140–190 words.

You have seen the following announcement on an international student website.

Articles wanted

Under pressure?

We know everyone out there is put under a lot of pressure sometimes! We want to read your articles about a time you were under a lot of stress and how you coped.

Send us your articles and we'll put the best on the website. Your experience could help others!

Write your **article**.

3 Read other students' articles. Whose way of coping do you admire most?

5 New words for

READING

that makes you feel great ...
achievement

awe·some /ˈɔːsəm $ ˈɒːs...*/
sive, serious, or difficult s...
worry, or fear: *an awesom...*
sweep of the scenery 2 ...
good: Their last con...
—awesomely *adv*

'awe-,stricken *adj* AWE...
awe·struck /ˈɔːstrʌk $ ...*

TOPIC
communication

READING FOCUS
how to use parts of speech

Exam task
Reading and Use of English,
Part 2: open cloze

WRITING FOCUS
how to write introductions
and conclusions in essays

Exam task
Writing, Part 1

1 Discuss these questions in pairs.

- What differences do you know between British English and American English? How do you think the languages influence each other?
- Why do some words fall out of fashion? Can you think of any words in your language which you use, but older people don't?

In Reading and Use of English, Part 2, you will read a text with gaps to complete. You have to think of a word which fits in each gap.

2 Read Rita's query. Can you help her?

9 comments ▼

RITA
I'm just doing some practice for Part 2 of the Reading and Use of English test. Anyone know what kind of words go in the gaps – nouns? verbs? Thanks, Rita ☺
Reply | Like | Posted September 29th at 7.32pm

Tyger
Hi Rita! Yeah, this task is all about grammar! Look at this article and the words in bold. It helped me understand what to focus on …
😎
Reply | Like | Posted September 29th at 9.35pm

3 Read the article that Tyger recommends. What reasons does the writer give for changes in British English?

Changing language

Language is in a constant state of change, and British English is no exception. Take **the** word 'Cheerio!' for example. It has been a British way to say goodbye for more than a century, but it's **dying out** as the English language evolves. These days, many young people simply say 'laters'. Or take the word 'marvellous'. At one time it was a common British word meaning 'very impressive', **but** over the last decade it's been overtaken by the American word 'awesome'.

So how and why do words come into and fall out of fashion? The influence of US culture is only **one** explanation for why popular words in British English **may** change or even stop being used over time. 'Awesome' is the obvious example, but also 'fortnight' – a term not used in the US – is currently falling out of fashion in British English, and in some cases **has** been replaced by the phrase 'two weeks'.

New conventions also spark new words. As old innovations are replaced by new ones, the words **which** described them also disappear and are replaced. So it's out with the 'Walkman' (a cassette player from the 80s) and in with MP4 players!

Then there's the influence of social media. Text messages and emails have reduced words for easy convenience, with acronyms like ICYMI ('in case you missed **it**') becoming words in their own right. Where 'friend' was once a noun, we now 'friend someone **on** Facebook' and where we used to 'love' something, now we're 'loving it'!

4 Look at the words in bold in the article. Write down which part of speech each one is, then compare your answers in pairs.

> adverb | ~~article~~ | auxiliary verb | conjunction | determiner | modal verb | phrasal verb | preposition | pronoun | relative pronoun

a the ......*article*......
b dying out ....
c but ....
d one ....
e may ....
f has ....
g which ....
h then ....
i it ....
j on ....

5a Work in pairs. Read each sentence and discuss what kind of word or phrase could go in each gap.

a Using the word 'brill' for brilliant has .... No one really uses it anymore.
b People who like languages enjoy learning new vocabulary and I am .... – I love new words!
c The word 'farewell' has been .... expressions like 'See you later'.

5b Use phrases from the text in exercise 3 to complete the sentences. You may have to change the verb form.

open cloze

1 Read the whole text first for **meaning**.

2 Read each gapped sentence, looking carefully at the words before and after the gap. Think about which **part of speech** is needed, e.g. verb, article, preposition.

3 Write the word you think goes in the gap. Then read the sentence again to make sure it makes **sense**.

Remember…

4 The words you need can be **grammatical** (e.g. a pronoun or auxiliary verb) or **lexical** (e.g. part of a fixed phrase such as *in fact* or *as far as I'm concerned*).

5 None of the missing words will be repeated in another gap.

6 You don't need to write your answers in order – **start** with the ones you find easier, then go back and complete the rest.

EXAM PRACTICE

1 Skim read the text about how the decision is made to include a new word in a dictionary.

2  Look at the example and think what part of speech the missing words might be. You have five minutes to complete this task.

Only write ONE word for each gap!

Example:

(0) FOR

How words get into the dictionary

Have you ever wondered how a word qualifies **(0)** _____ dictionary status? Only the recorded use of a word in

print or online over a period of time **(1)** _____ make Oxford University Press, publisher of the famous Oxford

Dictionaries, take serious notice and give it official recognition as a new word. 'When we have evidence of a new term

(2) _____ used in a variety of different sources,' says a spokeswoman, 'it becomes a candidate for inclusion in one

(3) _____ our dictionaries.'

Apparently, **(4)** _____ isn't enough to simply hear a term used in conversation or on TV. 'However, we do analyse

material from internet message boards and TV scripts,' **(5)** _____ spokeswoman continues. **(6)** _____ of the

latest phrases to have been added to the online Oxford Dictionaries site recently include 'Yolo', **(7)** _____ is an

acronym for 'You only live once', 'adorbs' (cute and adorable) and 'binge-watch' (to enthusiastically watch something on

TV). And **(8)** _____ a word enters the Oxford Dictionary, it never comes out!

---

3 Now read the text again. Complete each gap, using only one word in each gap.

WRITING

1 Answer this questionnaire and then compare your answers in pairs.

1 How many languages can you speak?

2 When and why did you start to learn it / them?

3 How often do you use this / these language(s)?

4 What do you remember about your first language learning experiences?

5 What advice would you give to people who are starting to learn another language?

6 Which other language(s) would you like to learn? Why?

WRITING FOCUS
how to write introductions and conclusions in essays
Exam task
Writing, Part 1

2a Work in pairs. Look at the pictures and describe what is happening.

2b Discuss in pairs. Which of these are good reasons for learning another language? Why?

* going on holiday
* learning about the culture of another country
* making friends from different countries
* moving to or working in another country
* taking school exams

5 New words for old

 Read the essay task and discuss the question in pairs. Look at the ideas to write about. What idea would you add to the list?

Is it better to learn another language at school or in the country where the language is spoken?

Notes

Write about:

1. motivation

2. opportunity

3. .... (your own idea)

4 **Read LolaB's post. What two pieces of advice would you give her?**

> 8 comments ▼
>
> **LolaB**
> I need to write an essay about language learning. I've got an essay plan which says: Introduction, Paragraph A, Paragraph B, (Paragraph C), and Conclusion. That's OK, but what sort of things go in an introduction or a conclusion? I need some advice here …
> Reply | Like | Posted July 1st at 12.37pm

5 **Read the essay on page 95. Which introduction and conclusion are better for this essay? Choose from A or B. Why?**

Introduction
A   In most countries students learn at least one foreign language at school and they usually go on to take exams in it. But is it better to go to the foreign country to learn the language? Common sense says that it's better to learn in the country! But is this really the case?
B   I'm going to tell you my opinions about learning a language at school or in a foreign country. It's an interesting question. Not everyone agrees with my opinion. Here is what I think.

Conclusion
A   In conclusion I think that the advantages of learning at school are that you get good teachers and you get good opportunities. When you learn for exams, you do a lot of hard work and you remember things for a long time. It's good to learn in another country too because you are motivated to learn then. Everyone can learn at school but not everyone can learn in a foreign country. So for these reasons I don't think I can give one answer to the question.
B   To conclude, I would say that there is no simple answer to the question. Learning a language in the foreign country is a natural way of learning a language but studying at school, on the other hand, gets us into good language learning habits. The answer? Study at school and visit the country to practise!

6 Read some summarising sentences from conclusions in essays about the best age to start learning another language. Choose the correct alternatives to complete the phrases.

a As we *can / could* see, while it may be a good idea to start learning another language at an early age, this is not necessarily always the *fact / case*.

b *On / In* balance I would *mention / say* that the earlier we start to learn a language the better.

c To *sum / summarise*, I think it's *fair / just* to say that it *depends / relies* on the child and on the language.

d So, *in contrast / in spite of* a few disadvantages I think there are lots of good *reasons / explanations* for starting to learn a language when you're young.

e To *conclusion / conclude* I think it's *clearly / clear* that there are both good and bad points.

4 WAYS to SMASH!

Writing, Part 1:

introductions and conclusions in essays

Introduction

1 Engage the reader immediately and tell them what to expect from the essay.

You could …

… ask a direct question.

… state a fact or outline a problem.

… give a common opinion or opposing ideas, e.g. *Some people think ... whereas others....*

Conclusion

2 Bring your ideas together briefly and give your own opinion.

3 Don't repeat all your ideas again – just summarise your opinions in one or two sentences, using connectors or linking phrases, e.g. *while, whereas, on the other hand*.

4 Give your final opinion or if you can't make a decision, say so!

EXAM PRACTICE

1 **Read the essay task and discuss your ideas in pairs.**

In your English class you have been talking about language learning. Now, your English teacher has asked you to write an essay.

Write an essay using **all** the notes and giving reasons for your point of view.

Is it better to speak one foreign language very well or to speak several languages a little?

Notes

Write about:

1. work

2. travelling

3. .... (your own idea)

Always make an essay plan to help organise your essay.

2 **Plan and then write your essay in 140–190 words.**

READING

TOPIC
innovation

READING FOCUS
how to change word forms

Exam task
Reading and Use of English,
Part 3: word formation

WRITING FOCUS
how to structure an email;
giving advice and making
suggestions

Exam task
Writing, Part 2: informal
email

1 **Look at the pictures. Discuss these questions in pairs.**

• Do you recognise the people in these pictures? What are they famous for creating?

• Do you think of yourself as a creative person? What kind of things do you create?

• What do you think has been the greatest invention or innovation in your lifetime?

• What do you think the phrase 'lightbulb moment' means?

In Reading and Use of English, Part 3 you will read a text with words missing. There is a prompt word for each of the gaps, which you have to change in order to complete the gaps accurately.

2 **Read the posts. Can you answer TinyD's question?.**

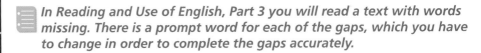
7 comments ▼

TinyD
Hi guys. Can you help me? What kind of changes do I have to make to the prompt words in Reading & Use of English, Part 3?
Reply | Like | Posted July 31st at 11.32am

Ed
Hi TinyD I was wondering the same thing and then I found this word formation exercise. Hope it helps!
Reply | Like | Posted August 2nd 7.15pm

3a Here's the exercise Ed recommends about word formation. Complete each sentence by making one or two changes to the word in brackets.

a Many people are of the belief that the wheel was the greatest ....*invention*............ of all time. (invent)

b Social media has .... not only our daily lives but the business world too. (revolution)

c No one's certain when the plough came into .... , but it changed farming methods forever. (exist)

d The printing press quickly rose in .... as its benefits became known. (popular)

e Refrigeration was put to both domestic and .... use in the early 20th century. (industry)

f Technology has provided us with the ability to .... quickly and effectively. (communicative)

g Though we no longer use them, steam engines were .... important in their time. (incredible)

h Without the jet engine, we'd have been .... to travel long distances quickly. (ability)

3b Look at your answers again. What changes have taken place? Write the part of speech: *adjective, adverb, noun* or *verb*.

a INVENT (verb) → ....*invention (noun)*............

b REVOLUTION (noun) → ....

c EXIST (verb) → ....

d POPULAR (adjective) → ....

e INDUSTRY (noun) → ....

f COMMUNICATIVE (adjective) → ....

g INCREDIBLE (adjective) → ....

h ABILITY (noun) → ....

4 Add the headings to this group of common prefixes and endings. In pairs, choose two prefixes or endings from each group and find examples of words which use them, e.g. (*ir-*) *irresponsible, irrelevant*.

> adjective endings | adverb endings | noun endings | ~~prefixes~~ | verb endings

a ....*prefixes*............

dis-, im-, in-, il-, ir-, mis-, over-, re-, un-

b ....

-ful, -ous, -able, -ible, -less, -ial, -ly, -ar

c ....

-ed, -ise, -en, -ing, -fy

d ....

-ly, -ily

e ....

-tion, -ment, -er/-or, -ist, -ness, -sion, -ity, -ship

5 Read the *Smash It!* list on page 38. Look at TinyD's query again. How would you answer it now?

word formation

During the test

1 When you learn a **new** word, record all its possible forms, e.g. *believe, believing, believed, belief, disbelief* and think about how the words might be used in sentences.

During the test

2 Read the whole text first for **meaning**.

3 Look at each gapped sentence and the prompt word. Decide which **part of speech** is needed in the gap, and choose the form which fits the context grammatically, e.g. Do you need the past participle of a verb? Is it the singular or plural form? Make sure the sentence makes sense!

4 Sometimes you may need to make the opposite form by adding a **prefix**, e.g. *agreement / disagreement, responsible / irresponsible, patience / impatience.*

5 The part of speech may not always change, e.g. *reach (verb) → (is) reaching (verb).*

EXAM PRACTICE

Read the text about innovations in football stadiums in the USA. Use the word given in capitals at the end of some of the lines to form a word that fits in the gap in the same line. There is an example at the beginning.

Example:

(0) FASCINATING

The world's best football stadiums

For some, the most **(0)** .... aspect of watching football is
going to the stadium and cheering for their team. But recently, the number
of people **(1)** .... National Football League (NFL) games in
the USA has **(2)** .... Fans now watch games from home,
where they can view instant **(3)** .... of what's just happened,
surf the Internet and avoid **(4)** .... weather like the freezing
cold! To attract more fans to stadiums, NFL teams spent billions of
dollars last year making **(5)** ....
The Levi's stadium in California is one of the world's most
(6) .... advanced stadiums, with free wireless Internet and a
mobile app allowing fans to order food from their seats. The stadium
has a solar roof for the **(7)** .... of power and high-definition
(HD) video boards providing a clear view of the action. And in the future?
Expect cameras integrated into helmets so you can see the game from
the players' viewpoint, and microphones to hear the coach's pre-game
(8) ....

Prompt words
FASCINATE
ATTEND
DROP
PLAY
PLEASANT
IMPROVE
TECHNOLOGY
GENERATE
SPEAK

You will have to make ONE or TWO changes to the prompt word – but not more.

WRITING

1 Discuss these questions in pairs.

- When did someone last email you asking for advice or suggestions?
- What did you tell them?
- Did they act on your advice?

2 Read Alfie's email. What would you say to Alfie? Discuss in pairs.

Hi Salvatore

I need to pick your brains! I'm doing a project about great inventors, past and present, from different countries. Who would you suggest I include from your country and why? And where's the best place to get some reliable information about him or her? I do hope you can help me out!

Thanks,

Alfie

3 Now read Salvatore's reply. How useful is his advice?

Hi Alfie,

That sounds like a cool project! I'm a science geek and one of my favourite inventors is that scientist from your country, Alexander Graham Bell. I think you should include him.

A lot of people think Bell was American but, as you know, he was born in Edinburgh, Scotland. He did a lot of work in America in his later life, though. I think he'd be great for your project because he invented the telephone and that paved the way for so many other wonderful technological inventions which changed everyone's life completely! Where would we be without the phone?

There's a brilliant TV series about inventors that I watched recently. One of the programmes is all about Bell. If you go online, you can probably find it. There's also a good website about inventors and their inventions. It's called *www. inventorswelove.com*

I hope that's helped. Send me a copy of your project when you've finished it. I'd love to read it!

Hope to hear from you soon,

Salvatore

WRITING FOCUS
how to structure an email; giving advice and making suggestions

Exam task
Writing, Part 2: informal email

THEN... NOW...

4 Read these posts and the *Smash It!* list. Now read Salvatore's email again. What has he done well? What could he improve?

> **16 comments ▼**
>
>
> **Frankie**
> I missed the class on writing emails! Were there any notes??
> Reply | Like | Posted January 7th at 9.46pm

> **17 comments ▼**
>
>
> **Mia_1**
> It was a really useful class. Here's a *Smash It!* list to help you.
> Reply | Like | Posted January 7th at 9.52pm

5 WAYS to SMASH!

Writing, Part 2: writing informal emails

1 Answer the question! Always read the question carefully and underline the important points you need to include. Often there will be more than one.

2 Refer to the email you've received, e.g. thank the person, ask them how they are or reply to their questions.

3 Don't just write one long paragraph! Divide your email into logical paragraphs.

4 You often need to use a function, e.g. giving advice, making suggestions or recommending something. Make sure you know some useful expressions for this.

5 Finish your email properly, e.g. add some interesting information about yourself, ask the other person a question or say you hope for an email back soon.

5 Add phrases from Salvatore's email to the useful phrases below.

Referring to previous email:	Giving advice and making suggestions:	Closing an email:
Lovely to hear from you.	Why don't you ...?	I'd better finish now because ...
Thanks for your email.	If I were you, I'd ...	Sorry, I've got to go now because ...
Well done on your results.	A good idea might be to ...	Don't forget to ...
What a great weekend!	How about ...?	I'm looking forward to ...
....	You could always ...	Hope to hear from you soon.
	....	....
	....	....

EXAM PRACTICE

1 Work in pairs. Read the advice about getting ideas. Do you ever do these things? Can you suggest any other ways of getting ideas?

Need to get some ideas but your mind's a blank?

1 Change your activity. Go for a walk, phone a friend or watch some TV.

2 Change your space. Go into a different room or place to work.

3 Daydream. Close your eyes and let your mind wander.

4 Brainstorm. Just write down any ideas you have in any order.

5 Get a good night's sleep. Often your brain continues to work on a problem when you're asleep and you might wake up with the answer!

2

Read the exam task. You have 40 minutes to plan and then write your email in 140–190 words.

You have received an email from your English friend, Alice.

From: Alice

Subject: Help!

I hope your course is still going well. I need your advice! I've got to come up with an idea for an original short story as part of my Creative Writing course and I've got writer's block. I can't think of anything. What do you do when your mind's a blank? Help!

Thanks,

Alice

Write your **email**.

READING

HONG KONG: THE BASICS

Location:	Hong Kong consists of 263 islands on the south-east coast of China.
Population:	7.24 million
Languages:	Cantonese and English (Hong Kong was under British rule between 1842 and 1997.)
Landmarks:	Victoria Peak (highest mountain in Hong Kong), Victoria Bay (largest harbour in China)
Activities:	tai chi (martial art) and yum cha (drinking tea)
Food:	Dim sum is a popular dish – small dumplings filled with meat or vegetables – often served with tea as part of yum cha.

TOPIC
location and lifestyle

READING FOCUS
how to rewrite sentences

Exam task
Reading and Use of English, Part 4: key word transformation

WRITING FOCUS
how to organise and link ideas in an essay

Exam task
Writing, Part 1

1 **Discuss these questions in pairs.**

- What do you know about Hong Kong?
- Have you ever visited Hong Kong?
- What do you like to do when you visit a city?

2 **Read the information about Hong Kong. In pairs, talk about 'the basics' of where you live.**

In Reading and Use of English, Part 4 you will read pairs of sentences. You have to complete the second sentence so that it means the same as the first. You will be given one word to help you, which you must include in the second sentence.

3a Work in pairs. Read what Cheng says about living in Hong Kong. Can you think of a different way to say the parts of the sentences in bold?

'When you hear the words Hong Kong, **you think of skyscrapers and boats** in the harbour.'

'**The views from Victoria Peak are amazing!**'

'**I get really annoyed by some tourists who visit**, particularly groups when they block your path.'

3b Use the phrases in the box to rewrite the parts of the sentences in bold.

come to mind | get on my nerves | take my breath away

a Skyscrapers and boats ....

b The views from Victoria Peak ....

c Some tourists who visit ....

4a Work in pairs. Read the posts then look at these pairs of sentences. What has changed in the second sentence of each pair?

5 comments ▼

RED97

Hey! Anyone know what kind of changes have to be made for the key word transformation exercises? Ta!

Reply | Like | Posted September 21st at 2.20pm

Ali B

Hi Red97! Here are some typical transformations! In the first one there is a grammatical change (direct → reported speech) and a lexical change using the phrase 'take your eyes off (something)'. Hope this helps!

Reply | Like | Posted September 21st at 3.05pm

1 'I can't stop looking at that view!' Wai Ling said.
  → Wai Ling said that she could not take her eyes off the view.

2 I wanted to do some tai chi, but I didn't have time.
  → I'd have done some tai chi if I'd had time.

3 Hearing about yum cha was very interesting for me.
  → I was very interested to hear about yum cha.

4 I think Hong Kong is the most beautiful city in China.
  → I don't think there are any other cities in China as beautiful as Hong Kong.

5 Tens of millions of tourists a year visit Hong Kong.
  → Hong Kong is visited by tens of millions of tourists a year.

6 People like relaxing in tea houses in Hong Kong.
  → Chilling out in tea houses is something people like doing in Hong Kong.

You may have to make a combination of grammatical and lexical changes for each sentence.

4b These grammar items are often practised in Reading and Use of English, Part 4. Match the items with the sentences above. Write the number of the sentence in the box.

a direct and indirect speech ☐

b phrasal verbs ☐

c conditional tenses ☐

d comparatives and superlatives ☐

e passive and active forms ☐

f gerund and infinitive forms ☐

Complete the second sentence so that it has a similar meaning to the first sentence. Use the word in bold but do not make any changes to this word.

1   The temples are known for their peaceful atmosphere by most people.

ASSOCIATE

Most people .... their peaceful atmosphere.

2   I think you ought to spend an afternoon at the Hong Kong Museum of History.

WERE

If I .... spend an afternoon at the Hong Kong Museum of History.

3   'I'll take you to the Lin Heung Tea House when you come to Hong Kong,' Mei promised me.

TAKE

Mei promised .... to the Lin Heung tea house when I visited Hong Kong.

4   I heard that a top Cantonese chef made the food at Feng's party last week.

APPARENTLY

The food at Feng's party last week .... a top Cantonese chef.

5   You can buy amazing things at the Temple Street night market, without spending too much money.

SPEND

You can buy amazing things at the Temple Street night market, and .... too much money.

6   Shanghai, where I used to live, is flatter than Hong Kong.

FLAT

Hong Kong .... Shanghai, where I used to live.

8 WAYS to SMASH!

Reading & Use of English, Part 4:

key word transformation

Before the test

1 Choose some interesting sentences from a website, book or magazine and try **rewriting** them using different grammar and vocabulary so that the meaning is the same.

2 Make a note of phrasal verbs and main verbs you come across which have **similar** meanings.

3 Keep a record of sayings and **idioms** in English.

4 **Practise** reporting what people say or writing passive forms of active sentences.

During the test

5 Make sure the **two** sentences mean the **same**.

6 Include the **key word** but DON'T make any changes to it!

7 Don't use more than five words to complete the second sentence.

8 Contractions (e.g. *don't, I've*) count as TWO words.

WRITING

1 Discuss in pairs. If you could live anywhere you wanted, where would it be and why? Think about:

- facilities - location - people - type of building

2 Read Deb's and Charlie's comments about where they live. Discuss these questions in pairs.

- What would they dislike if they had to swap homes?
- Which island would you prefer to live on? Why?

Charlie

'I live on the Isle of Skye and I just love the peace and beauty of it. Don't want to shout about it too much or everyone will want to come and live here – and that would spoil everything!'

Deb

'Nothing compares to living on the island of Manhattan! So cool, so much to do, such an exciting atmosphere! I wouldn't want to live anywhere else.'

WRITING FOCUS
how to organise and link ideas in an essay

Exam task
Writing, Part 1

3 Look at the essay task. Now read the exam candidate's answer on page 46. Does it include any of the points you mentioned in exercises 1 and 2?

Life in an urban environment is better than life in a rural location. Do you agree?

Write about:

1. health

2. cost

3. .... (your own idea)

4a Read Saffy's post. What ideas can you give Saffy?

7 comments ▼

Saffy505

Hi people! Homework today is another essay. Last time I got a low mark because my sentences were too simple. I can use 'and' and 'but' to make them longer but that gets boring. Any more ideas??

Reply | Like | Posted December 8th at 6.13pm

4b Read this essay written by an exam candidate. Underline linking words and phrases that Saffy could use to improve her writing. There is an example to help you.

Many people think that living in an urban environment is better than living somewhere quieter but is that necessarily true?

Pollution can be a problem for your health. Constant traffic produces quite severe air pollution which is not good for us. In addition to this, traffic can cause a lot of noise pollution, although it is not the only cause. Crowds of people and noisy neighbours can also be disruptive.

Another important point is cost. Sometimes the price of accommodation in urban areas can be prohibitive, whereas the same money could get a bigger property in the countryside.

A good point about living in built-up areas is the convenience. Journeys to work are shorter and therefore it's easy to get to theatres, shops and other amenities. There's often a lively, exciting atmosphere which many people like.

To conclude, I must say that much depends on the area, as well as on people's personalities. However, I have to admit that for me the negative points of life in an urban environment definitely outweigh the positive ones. I enjoy the peace and quiet of a rural location.

4c Add any appropriate words and phrases you underlined to these lists.

Adding	Contrasting	Giving cause and result	Using relative pronouns
and	but	so	who
moreover	while	as a result	where
....	despite / in spite of	consequently	....
....	....	as a consequence	....
....	....	....	....

5 Complete the sentences in your own words.

a I love pedestrianised city centres where ....

b My favourite house was the house I grew up in. Despite...

c My parents moved house a lot when I was young. As a result, ...

d We have a fantastic shopping mall near us which ....

e I wouldn't like to live in the countryside, although ....

f Most people like peace and quiet, whereas ....

6 WAYS to SMASH!

Writing, Part 1:

organising and linking ideas

1 Always give yourself time to plan and organise your ideas for your essay. Make notes about the different points to include.

2 Divide your essay into clear paragraphs to deal with different ideas.

3 Use words and phrases that show the reader what you're going to be talking about, e.g. *One problem can be ... Another important point is ... To conclude ...*

4 Use linking words and phrases to join sentences.

It depends on the area **as well as** on people's personalities.

5 Link ideas across sentences with connecting words and phrases.

It can cause health problems. **In addition to this**, it can cause noise pollution.

6 Use relative pronouns to link sentences and make comments.

There is an exciting atmosphere **which** can attract lots of people.

EXAM PRACTICE

1 **Which of the islands on page 45 would you have preferred to live on when you were a child? Why?**

2 **Read the exam task and add a third idea. Compare your ideas in pairs.**

In your English class you have been talking about cities.

Now, your English teacher has asked you to write an essay.

Write an essay using **all** the notes and give reasons for your point of view.

Is it better for a child to grow up in a rural or urban location?

Notes

Write about:

1. education

2. free time activities

3. .... (your own idea)

3 **SMASH! the clock!** You have **40 minutes** to make notes and plan your essay. Then write your essay in 140–190 words. Try to use some of the linking words and phrases from the unit.

READING

1 Look at the pictures of people doing challenges to raise money for charity. Discuss these questions in pairs.

- What are the people in the pictures doing?
- Why do you think they have taken the photographs?
- Have you ever done anything to raise money for a charity?

2 Read the title and introduction to an article. What kind of information do you think the article will include? What will the writer investigate?

Charity Challenges

It was the craze that took over your Facebook feed, but was the ice bucket challenge the best way to make money for charity? Jen Brownrigg investigates.

3a Read the first paragraph of the article on page 49. Answer the question.

How did Toby feel about having done the ice bucket challenge?

A proud that he had encouraged other people to take the challenge

B pleased that so many people had benefited from his actions

C regretful that he hadn't raised more money for charity

D surprised by how much he had enjoyed the experience

3b Check the answer to the question. Which part of the text gives you the answer? Underline it. Why are the other options incorrect?

In Reading and Use of English, Part 5 you have to answer multiple-choice questions which have four options to choose from. Only one option is correct. You may be asked to answer questions on opinion, attitude, purpose, main idea and detail.

Charity Challenges

1   Do you remember when everyone, from your next-door neighbour to David Beckham, seemed to be doing the 'ice bucket challenge' – pouring a bucket of ice water over their head, posting a video of themselves doing it, and nominating others to do the same? More than 2.4 million videos were posted on Facebook in the UK. They raised huge amounts of money for a charity to help people with motor neurone disease. As Toby, 22, puts it, 'I got the opportunity to do something silly, the charity got a bit more money and my girlfriend got the chance to pour cold water over me – everyone was a winner – how cool is that? The water was so cold it took my breath away – I'm not sure I'll repeat the experience any time soon!'

EXAM PRACTICE

1 **Look at these questions. Match each question with the kind of information it is asking about.**

1 What attitude does Michael Wilkinson express towards online challenges?
2 What is the writer doing in paragraph 2?
3 How did Anthony Carbajal feel about the outcome of his own ice bucket video?

a the purpose of one part of the text
b an individual's beliefs
c an individual's emotional reaction

2a **Read paragraphs 2 and 3 and answer the questions on page 50.**

Charity Challenges

2   Although many people had great fun completing the challenge, not everyone was a fan. Some worried about wasted water, others worried about the ethics. 'What is wrong with quietly giving money to charity?' asked journalist Michael Wilkinson. He argues that online challenges like these are less about giving money and more about celebrities grabbing attention or people showing off in front of their friends without really understanding the charity. In fact, only half of those taking the ice bucket challenge mentioned the name of the charity in their videos. Many people seemed more interested in getting 'likes' and comments on their posts than helping the charities. And worse still, it is said that not everyone actually donated the money they'd promised.

3   So was it worth it? For one ice bucket video-maker Anthony Carbajal, it was. After he did the challenge in his video, Anthony announced: 'My grandmother and my mother had motor neurone disease. And now I have it.' Anthony's video went viral and was soon watched by over 16 million people worldwide and made over a million for charity. 'This diagnosis is so hard, but with so many strangers reaching out to me with their love and support, and knowing that more people now know about this disease; my heart is just overwhelmed,' he said.

Read the questions and options carefully before you read the text.

8 Fundraising revolution

1 What attitude does Michael Wilkinson express towards online challenges?

    A   confusion about why some of the videos attracted negative feedback

    B   doubt about it being an improvement on traditional methods of donating

    C   concern that charities do not always receive the funds participants raise

    D   disapproval of the way charities are promoted by well-known people

2 What is the writer doing in paragraph 2?

    A   suggesting ways in which participants could promote charities

    B   clarifying reasons for the behaviour of certain participants

    C   supporting a point of view about online challenges

    D   criticising others' objections to online challenges

3 How did Anthony Carbajal feel about the outcome of his own ice bucket video?

    A   convinced that it would help other people promote similar issues

    B   amazed by the number of similar stories he heard about as a result

    C   uncertain about whether his message had been properly interpreted

    D   grateful that it had raised greater awareness of a physical condition

2b Now check your answers and underline the part of the text where this information is found. Does the article use the same words? If not, how are they different?

3 Read the final part of the article. Do you think the challenge was a good way to raise money for charity? Discuss in pairs.

4   The ice bucket challenge was not the first or only online challenge. After a fire at a dogs' home in Manchester, animal-lover Joe Farrar set up a 'dog selfie' Facebook page. This time people posted photographs of themselves with their pet dog and gave money to help rebuild the dogs' home. Another trend that took the Internet by storm was the 'no make-up selfie'. Facebook was full of photographs of women wearing no make-up and nominating their friends to do the same. It was a huge success and raised £8 million in just six days.

4 WAYS to SMASH!

Reading & Use of English, Part 5:

detail, opinion, purpose, main idea and attitude

1 Some questions require you to read the whole paragraph or part of the text to gain a **general** understanding. Others require careful reading of **specific** words and phrases.

2 Opinion and attitude questions: look for phrases, expressions and quotes in the text which indicate **feelings** and **opinions**.

3 Purpose questions may start with phrases like *What is the writer doing …?* or *What is the writer's aim / purpose …?* Read the whole paragraph to understand the writer's **message**.

4 The words used in the text and options may be different.

I hated every minute of it! / He didn't enjoy it at all.
I'd do it all again tomorrow! / She is keen to repeat the experience.

WRITING

1 **Look at the pictures and discuss these questions in pairs.**

- What type of voluntary work can people do in your area?
- Do you think everyone should be encouraged to do volunteer work?
- Have you ever done any volunteer work? What did you do?
- What kind of voluntary work would you like to do and why?

WRITING FOCUS
language and content of a report

Exam task
Writing, Part 2: report

2 **Work in pairs. Read Ella's post and answer these questions.**

- Have you ever written a report?
- What do people usually write reports about?
- What advice would you give Ella?

12 comments ▼

UmbrElla
There's a report in the Writing test and I've never written a report even in MY language! What do I need to do?
Reply | Like | Posted October 30th at 4.00pm

POLO
Hey Ella! Here's a report I wrote recently. Let me know if it helps you. Have a look at the Smash It! list too!

Reply | Like | Posted November 1st at 3.14pm

3 Work in pairs. Read Polo's report and the *Smash It!* list on page 53. Find examples of the seven points from the *Smash It!* list in Polo's report.

To: Professor Talford
From: Paul Martin
Subject: College volunteering activities

Introduction
The purpose of this report is to outline the volunteering activities that students at the college have taken part in this term and to recommend which should be organised again next year.

College run
Sixty-five students helped disabled children and adults to complete the Big College Run in April. A large amount of money was also raised for new equipment through sponsorship and donations on the day.

Computer skills
Ninety-five students took part in the 'computer development skills weekend' in May. Local elderly people were invited to the college to be taught simple computer skills that would help them to keep in touch with friends and family electronically.

Sponsored litter clean-up
On 25th May students cleared up beaches and areas of local countryside. For each bag of rubbish the students collected, the council donated an amount of money to a children's play area.

Conclusion
This summer students should be proud of having helped the local community in many ways. All the events were successful, but I would definitely recommend that the litter clean-up event is repeated next year. Not only did it raise money for people in need, but it also helped the environment.

7 WAYS to SMASH!

Writing, Part 2:

reports

1. Divide the report into clear sections and give each one a **heading**.
2. Always give an **introduction** to explain the purpose or aim of the report.
3. Use the **conclusion** to give a summary and make a recommendation.
4. Don't use informal language with contractions and colloquialisms.
5. Use some **passive** verb forms – a report should be quite impersonal.
6. Use some more **advanced** structures if you can.
7. A report should include facts and **details**.

4a Complete the phrases for making more formal recommendations with the words in the box.

| definitely | idea | recommendation | should | suggest | would |

a I would .... recommend repeating this activity.
b We .... consider trying something new.
c It might be a good .... to involve local school children.
d It .... benefit everyone if we raised even more money next year.
e To make improvements I would .... bringing the date of the run forward.
f My .... would be to organise another activity in late summer.

4b Work in pairs. Use the phrases to make recommendations in answer to these questions.

- Which local charities or projects would you raise money for?
- How would you attract volunteers to help the local community?

EXAM PRACTICE

1 Work in pairs. Read the exam task and discuss some fun volunteering events you could write about in the report.

Your town wants to hold a special volunteer week this summer.

The town council has asked you to write a report. Your report should:

- include some ideas of volunteering activities suggested by your fellow students
- recommend which activity the council should choose and why

2

You have **40 minutes** to plan and complete this task. Write your report in 140–190 words.

3 Compare reports in class and find out which volunteer activity most people recommend.

READING

TOPIC
relationships

READING FOCUS
how to understand meaning from context: implication, tone and references to language

Exam task
Reading and Use of English, Part 5: multiple choice

WRITING FOCUS
how to use a good range of language

Exam task
Writing, Part 2: article

---

1 Look at the pictures. Discuss these questions in pairs.

- What is your first impression of the people in the pictures?
- Why do you think humans stereotype other people?
- Do you think there's any truth to stereotypes?
- Is stereotyping helpful or harmful?

 In Part 5 you have to answer multiple-choice questions which show your understanding of the context.

---

4 comments ▼

Dude

Hello everyone! I've just found out that some of the questions in Part 5 ask about the writer's message and opinions, or refer to language in the text. Sounds tricky!
Reply | Like | Posted December 2nd at 2.40pm

MAGIC
Hey Dude! These questions aren't as complicated as they sound. You can tell what the writer thinks by the words he / she uses. So he / she might say something positive, like 'It's fair to say that …' or something negative, such as 'I'm not sure whether …' All the information's in the text, you just need to read carefully!
Reply | Like | Posted December 3rd at 3.00pm

stereotype?

2a Read the title to the article. What information do you think the article will include?

What are stereotypes?

1 Stereotypes are widely held but very general, simplified opinions about other people. They may be accurate, harmless, wrong or even damaging. So why do we do it? The use of stereotypes is a major way to simplify our social world. They reduce the amount of processing we need to do when we meet someone new. By stereotyping, we infer that a person has a whole range of characteristics typical to all members of a group. This leads to social categorisation and is one reason for prejudice – creating a 'them versus us' mentality. Many stereotypes tend to convey a negative impression of the group being described.

2b Read the first paragraph of the article and answer the multiple-choice question. Discuss the reasons for your answer in pairs. Refer back to the text where possible.

Do you think the writer conveys

a a mainly negative attitude towards stereotyping?

b a mainly positive attitude towards stereotyping?

c a balanced attitude?

2c Which of the following are other ways to ask the question in exercise 2b? Tick all that apply.

a Which definition of stereotyping does the writer agree with? ☐

b What is the writer's opinion of stereotyping? ☐

c How does the writer feel about stereotyping? ☐

3 Read the next part of the article. Look at the words in bold in the article. Which parts of speech are they?

What are stereotypes?

2 Many of us start to use stereotypes at school – the nerds, the cool kids, the hot kids – we know all the different **ones** by heart. While pigeonholing others seems to be part of basic human nature, labels seem to be used most often in high school, and lead to many 'cliques' or sub-groups.

3 Looks, clothes, personal traits and interests are all aspects which, on the surface of it, make us different from our contemporaries. Students pounce on **these** in order to categorise others. 'When you're a social animal, you need to understand who is a member of your pack, and who is a member of a different pack,' says psychology professor, John Dovidio.

4 A girl may dress all in black and you call her an 'emo' or 'goth'. But maybe, deep down inside, she just likes black and is actually cheerful and bubbly. She has the same interests as you – (the 'cool kid') – but she just dresses differently. The pitfall of typecasting is that **it** involves using labels which are merely shells containing assumptions. It makes one wonder why people see only a narrow view of a complicated human being.

4 Match the words in bold in the text with what they refer to.

1 ones   **a** typecasting

2 these   **b** aspects of ourselves

3 it   **c** stereotypes

9 Hardwired to stereotype?

5 Read the next part of the article and underline the sentences where you find the writer's own point of view.

What are stereotypes?

5 Are humans born to stereotype, then? Many psychologists think that our brains are subconsciously hardwired to stereotype. As Dovidio explains, in a world of survival of the fittest, animals have to make rapid judgements about their predators. 'They need to distinguish friend from enemy,' he says. As examples, Dovidio points out that some chimpanzees attack chimps of the same species who are not part of their group. And some fish attack their own kind simply because they weren't hatched in the same lake. If someone or something is hardwired to do a particular thing,

line 11 they automatically do it and cannot change that behaviour.

6 When it comes to humans, Dovidio says that even if we think we don't stereotype others, we do. 'We categorise immediately and without thinking.' And we stereotype others not just on their appearance, how they dress or act, but – wrongly – on their race and sex too.

7 Student stereotypes may have special meanings, as teens are in the process of forming their own identity and figuring out who they feel most comfortable with. To some extent, stereotyping offers a sense of order, direction and connection to the close friends they make over time. But it's too simple to make assumptions that 'they'– teenagers in other groups – are alike or different from 'us'. It's easy to throw a group of people into a bucket and judge them as a whole; it's much more difficult to look at each person as an individual. On the other hand, Jim, another high-school student, says, 'by labelling people we're actually highlighting similarities not differences. If we didn't stereotype, it would make many things today impossible. Think of marketing studies focused on specific audiences, or clubs for people of like interests or hobbies.'

REMEMBER!

The writer may not use words like *I think* or *In my opinion*. Look for other ways in which the writer offers their point of view.

---

4 WAYS to SMASH!

Reading & Use of English, Part 5:

understanding implication, tone and reference

1 Look for **clues** in the text which offer the writer's own opinion.

2 You may need to think about the **whole** text and the writer's attitude towards its main arguments. Look out for positive and negative words, and phrases for agreeing and disagreeing.

3 Read carefully – what is the writer suggesting? Don't make assumptions – it's **all** in the text!

4 If you're asked what a word or phrase refers to, remember that it could refer to something before or after it. The **context** will provide you with enough information to help you answer.

EXAM PRACTICE

1 Look at these explanations. Then read questions 1–4 in exercise 2 and decide which kind of question each one is.

a Questions about tone ask about the general feeling of the whole text or section of text.

b Implication questions ask about what the writer is suggesting, but not saying directly.

c Reference questions ask about the meaning of words or phrases.

2  Read questions 1–4 again. Scan the complete article (on pages 55 and 56) and underline where you think each answer is. You have **five minutes** for this task.

1 What does 'it' mean in line 11?

  A behaviour
  B be hardwired
  C a particular thing
  D someone or something

2 What is implied in paragraph 6?

  A Dovidio's theories may not be correct.
  B People cannot help the way they react to others.
  C We make judgements about ourselves as well as other people.
  D Dovidio has correctly identified the kinds of stereotypes we make.

3 In paragraph 7, the writer expresses a belief that teenagers

  A are afraid of being put into the wrong social group by their peers.
  B lack interest in people who appear to be different from themselves.
  C make negative judgements about others in order to make themselves feel better.
  D rely on stereotypes because it's easier than making an effort to understand others.

4 What is the overall attitude of the article?

  A regretful that humans are not always kind to one another
  B critical of the way humans make judgements about others
  C sympathetic to the reasons why humans stereotype others
  D positive about a future without negative stereotyping

Keep an open mind when you first read through the questions. Work out which options are NOT correct first!

3 For questions 1–4, choose the answer (A, B, C or D) which you think fits best according to the text.

4 Discuss in pairs. How can we avoid labelling new people who we meet?

WRITING

Exam task
Writing, Part 2: article

 Work in pairs. Think about a good friend and discuss these questions.

a How long have you known him / her?

b How did you get to know him / her?

c How long did it take for him / her to become a good friend?

d How important are these things for a good friendship? Why?

- friends in common
- similar ages
- similar aims and ambitions
- similar backgrounds
- similar interests
- similar strengths and weaknesses

2a Read K8's post and her article on page 96 and underline words and phrases you think she repeats.

---

8 comments ▼

K8
Hi guys! Here's an article I've written about friendship. Has anyone got any suggestions about how to improve it? Do you think I use the same words too much?
Reply | Like | Posted December 13th at 5.15pm

2b Compare in pairs. Have you underlined the same words?

3 Rewrite the sentences using the alternatives in the box instead of the words in bold.

| but | close to | doing | for instance | for me | issues | thoughts about | true | views | while |

a For example, Lorrie's **opinions** about what's right or wrong and her **attitudes** to **things** like celebrity culture are **similar to** mine.

b The basis of a good friendship **in my opinion** is firstly to be supportive.

c In my opinion a **real** friend is someone like my mate Lorrie.

d I'm into books and I'm studying Literature at university **whereas** Lorrie loves sports and is **studying** Sports Psychology.

e Although we sometimes disagree, we are still friends afterwards.

4 The words in italics in the following sentences are often over-used by students. Work in pairs and think of words to replace them with.

a I have a *nice* friend.

b I *got* a letter from my friend yesterday.

c We had a *nice* meal together.

d I *like* romantic novels.

e She's *very* kind.

f The weather is *very bad* today.

g Lorrie has *lots of* online friends.

h It's a *big* problem.

5 K8 has used a good range of structures in her article. Find examples of:

a present simple

b present continuous

c present perfect

d past simple

e future simple

5 WAYS to SMASH!

articles

Writing, Part 2:

1 Try to avoid repeating the same words and phrases in your writing. Think of synonyms for adjectives, verbs and phrases, e.g. *real / true, studying / doing, for example / for instance.*

2 Learn different functional phrases to avoid repetition, e.g. *in my opinion, for me, in my view.*

3 Use a range of linking words, e.g. *whereas / while, although / but / however.*

4 Try to find alternative words to use instead of (or as well as) common words, e.g. *nice: pleasant, delicious, kind; get: receive, own, have.*

5 Use a wide choice of tenses and other structures to show your grammatical range.

EXAM PRACTICE

1 Read the exam task for K8's article and then plan and write your own article in 140 –190 words.

You have seen this announcement on an international student website.

Articles wanted

A friend for life

Friends are important for all of us. We are looking for articles about a particularly good friend of yours. How did you get to know each other? Are you similar or different? What qualities make him / her a great friend?

Send in your **articles** and we'll put the best ones on the website.

2 Share your articles with other students. Vote on which one(s) should go on the website.

READING

1 **Look at the pictures. Discuss these questions in pairs.**

- What are the people doing in each picture?
- What could the consequences of their actions be?

2 **Look at this questionnaire. What other questions could you add to it?**

Do you need a digital detox?

Are you spending too much time glued to your digital devices? If you answer 'yes' to more than half of these questions, it may be time to take a break!

1 Do you own more than two digital devices?

2 Do you prefer talking to people online rather than face-to-face?

3a **Look at the first paragraph of an article entitled 'Digital detox'. What kind of information do you think is missing at (0)? Choose a, b or c. Work in pairs and give reasons for your answer.**

a where Julianne is
b what Julianne ought to be doing
c what Julianne can see on the screen

It's eight-thirty on a Wednesday evening and Julianne sits hunched over her laptop. (0) _____ Instead, she's replying to a group invite on Facebook. Then, just as Julianne clicks back to her Powerpoint slides, her friend Sally, who wants to cheer her up while she's working, sends a funny video of a monkey on a skateboard.

or dangerous?

3b **Read the missing sentence. Which words on the first paragraph indicate this is the correct option?**

She's under pressure to finish preparing a presentation for a work meeting first thing.

In Reading and Use of English, Part 6, you have to complete a gapped text. Six sentences have been removed from the text and you have to decide where they go.

4a **Read the next part of the text. Look at the gaps and predict what kind of information is missing.**

Julianne forwards the YouTube link to four other friends. Everyone starts swapping pictures on WhatsApp. It's nine o'clock and Julianne is trying to finalise her presentation, but an email pings on her smartphone – great new offers on her favourite clothing brand. **(1) _____**

Time is running out to finish off her presentation. But before she can proofread her slides, her friend Jen IMs her. It isn't good news. **(2) _____** By the time they finish chatting, it's almost midnight.

Julianne goes to bed, but she soon finds herself scrolling through her Twitter feed before switching off the light. During the night, she's woken up three times by her smartphone buzzing with texts and emails. Julianne oversleeps. **(3) _____** No wonder she's anxious: she hasn't checked through her presentation and if she doesn't hurry, she'll be late for work.

4b **Work in pairs. Write a possible sentence for each gap.**

6 WAYS to SMASH!

Reading & Use of English, Part 6:

gapped text

1 Read the **whole** text first, ignoring the spaces, to gain a **general** understanding.

2 Look at **each gap** and think about what information might be missing. Read the options to see if there is a similar idea.

3 Try putting each **possible option** into the gap to see if it fits. Read the sentences before and after the gap to help you decide. Make sure the sentence works in the context.

4 Look at the **clues** around each gap, e.g. linking words, pronouns, determiners, tenses. You can also look out for reasons, consequences, or similar and contrasting ideas.

5 If you get stuck, **move on** to another gap – you don't have to complete them in order!

6 Read each paragraph again to check that it makes **sense**.

1 Read the whole text again, starting on page 61, and choose from the sentences A–G the one which fits in each gap (1–6). Follow the advice in the *Smash It!* list.

Julianne's story is all too familiar. We're so bombarded with messages, posts, streams and emails that it can feel as if laptops and smartphones have overtaken our lives. **(4)** _____ And more troubling is a recent survey in which one in four people admits to spending more time online each day than asleep.

There is something totally compulsive about the Internet. Some people even suffer from anxiety known as FOMO which is when they are too scared to switch off their mobile phones for Fear Of Missing Out on something exciting or important. **(5)** _____ These include impaired memory, anxiety, disturbed sleep patterns and even depression.

But now some high-profile people are fighting back. Kathryn Parsons, CEO of Decoded, a fast-growing tech company, hit the headlines when she announced she was deleting her email account. 'When you say you've come off email, people's jaws drop,' she says. 'I just wanted to experiment with a new way of doing things. And it's worked really well.' **(6)** _____ She's now able to focus on her most important projects without being distracted and bogged down by messages that waste her time. These days if you want to contact Parsons you have to send her a text and hope she'll reply.

A   She eventually wakes up irritable.

B   She clicks on the link and can't resist browsing.

C   Wiping her email has made her a lot more productive.

D   According to the Daily Telegraph, the average person checks their phone every six and a half minutes.

E   This is precisely what she sets out to do.

F   But our addiction to technology can have unpleasant side effects.

G   The kids are driving her mad and she needs to let it all out.

Don't forget there's an extra sentence which doesn't fit in the text at all!

2 Read the final paragraph of the article. Discuss the questions in pairs.

- Why do you think people would be 'too scared to follow Parsons' example'?
- What 'small steps' could people take to make sure technology doesn't take over their lives?
- Could you do a digital detox?

In this hyper-connected world, most people would be too scared to follow Parsons' example. But we can all take small steps to ensure that we don't become overwhelmed by technology. As a journalist from the Huffington Post says: 'It's up to us to set boundaries. Isn't it exhausting to be online all the time?'

WRITING

1 **Read the extract from a TV guide. Discuss these questions in pairs.**

- Would you like to watch this programme? Why / Why not?
- What sort of information would you expect to find in a review of this programme?

> **9.00 Cyberbully** (drama starring Maisie Williams.)
> You think you're in control of your online life? Think again!
> Casey Jacobs is convinced that she is, but she's got a big shock coming.

2 **Read a student's review of the drama and discuss these questions.**

- Does the review contain the right kind of information?
- Does the review change your mind about whether you'd like to watch the programme or not? Why? / Why not?

Cyberbully

There was an absolutely brilliant TV drama last week on Channel 4. Did you see it? It was called 'Cyberbully' and starred the exceptionally talented Maisie Williams. It was set in a teenager's bedroom and involved no one else apart from the teenager and her computer. I was hooked from the very beginning.

'Cyberbully' follows one evening in the life of Casey Jacobs. Casey, just like many of us today, lives her life online. The drama shows what can happen when a simple, unintentionally cruel comment goes viral. We are never sure whether Casey is a victim or a bully and the story is full of twists and turns. The truth unfolds slowly and the tension builds to a dramatic climax.

In my opinion this was drama at its very best - gripping and compelling. It was extremely well directed, and the great storyline and script coupled with a superb performance by Maisie Williams made it compulsive viewing. What I particularly liked was the way that moral questions about cyberbullying had no black or white answers. I loved it!

3 Look at a teacher's comments about the review. Underline examples of what she's referring to in the review on page 63.

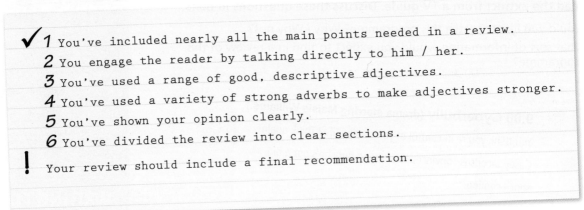

✓ **1** You've included nearly all the main points needed in a review.

2 You engage the reader by talking directly to him / her.

3 You've used a range of good, descriptive adjectives.

4 You've used a variety of strong adverbs to make adjectives stronger.

5 You've shown your opinion clearly.

6 You've divided the review into clear sections.

! Your review should include a final recommendation.

4 Read these recommendations and decide which would be best to finish the review.

a If you like good drama, then you must see this. If you miss it, check it out on catch-up TV later! You won't be disappointed.

b Unfortunately this drama doesn't live up to the hype. I would give it a miss.

c I would certainly not recommend this to anyone who has no interest in modern communication technology.

d This is an excellent drama and a 'must-see' for anyone who does a lot of social networking. It could change your life.

5a Read Olly's post. Is DJ_Blake's reply helpful?

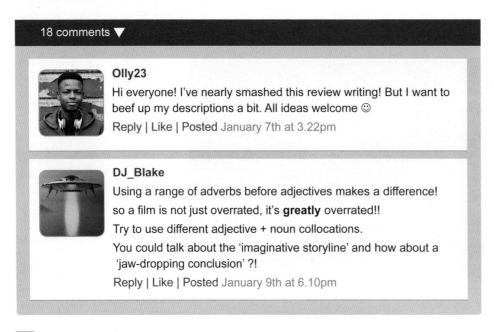

18 comments ▼

Olly23
Hi everyone! I've nearly smashed this review writing! But I want to beef up my descriptions a bit. All ideas welcome ☺
Reply | Like | Posted January 7th at 3.22pm

DJ_Blake
Using a range of adverbs before adjectives makes a difference!
so a film is not just overrated, it's **greatly** overrated!!
Try to use different adjective + noun collocations.
You could talk about the 'imaginative storyline' and how about a 'jaw-dropping conclusion' ?!
Reply | Like | Posted January 9th at 6.10pm

5b Now add examples from the review on page 63 to the lists.

adverb + adjective:	adjective + noun collocations:
greatly overrated	imaginative storyline
unnecessarily long	jaw-dropping conclusion
surprisingly slow	complicated plot
a	d ....
b	e ....
c	f ....

6 WAYS to SMASH! Writing, Part 2:

review

1 Include all the **points** asked for in the question.

2 Divide your review into **clear** paragraphs / sections:
- the name and some basic information
- more information, e.g. a summary of the story
- why you like or dislike it
- a summary of your opinion and your recommendation

3 DON'T go into too much detail – you don't have space or time!

4 Remember your target reader – your style should be **appropriate**.

5 **Engage** the reader by sometimes talking to them directly.

6 Use a **variety** of adverbs and adjectives to make your description more vivid.

EXAM PRACTICE

1 **SMASH! the clock!** Choose one of the exam tasks. You have **40 minutes** to make notes and plan your review. Then write your review in 140–190 words.

You see this notice on a student website.

> **Reviews wanted**
>
> Have you seen something brilliant on TV recently? Or maybe something you thought was terrible? Write a review of the programme for the website, explaining what sort of programme it was, how you felt about it and why you would or wouldn't recommend it to other students.

You see this announcement on an English-language website.

> **Send us a review!**
>
> We're looking for reviews of recent films that our readers have seen. Write a review of a film that has impressed you in a good or bad way, and give your reasons.
>
> Send it to us and we will put the best online for all to see.

When you talk about the actions in a film or book, use the present simple e.g. *Casey opens the email but it isn't from her friend.*

2 Work in pairs. Swap reviews. Would you like to watch the programme your partner has reviewed?

READING

30 places to see before you're 30

Got the travel bug? Here are our top 30 travel destinations for modern adventurers!

 **1 City break:** combine chilling on the beach with shopping, sightseeing and nightlife in Barcelona, Spain.

 **2 Surfer central:** polish your skills in the Atlantic waves off the south-west coast of Morocco.

 **3 Adrenaline adventure:** go skiing, trekking, climbing or white-water rafting in the Rocky Mountains, USA.

TOPIC
travel

READING FOCUS
how to understand detail, opinion and attitude

Exam task
Reading and Use of English, Part 7: multiple matching

WRITING FOCUS
how to use tenses in story writing

Exam task
Writing, Part 2 (*First for Schools*): story

1 Work in pairs. Read the introduction to a magazine article and discuss these questions in pairs.

- Which of these places would you most like to visit and why?
- What places would you put at the top of the '30 places' list?
- Why do people travel?
- Does how you travel make a difference to what you learn about a country?
- Is travelling the best way to learn about the world and other cultures?

In Part 7 you will read a series of short texts on the same subject or a longer text divided into sections. You have to match questions to the texts or sections in which the information is given.

2 Match the verbs and definitions.

1 state — a to say what something / someone is like
2 mention   b to make something clear by giving more information
3 explain   c to say clearly and carefully
4 describe   d to show an idea / feeling without saying it directly
5 suggest   e to refer to something / someone

3 Look at these words and phrases that you may see in the questions for Part 7. Which words describe how someone is feeling? What do the other words mean? Discuss in pairs.

anxious | amused | appreciates | attempted | discovered | doubtful | emphasises | values

4a Read the questions and decide which requires you to understand detail or specific information (D) or opinion, feeling or attitude (O). Circle D or O.

1 Which person did not enjoy their study trip abroad?   D / O
2 Which paragraph provides a review of an eco-tourism spot?   D / O
3 Which student felt relieved when their journey was over?   D / O
4 Which part describes an unusual type of accommodation?   D / O
5 Which section provides an example of a transport problem?   D / O
6 Which teenager was annoyed by a delay in getting to a holiday resort? D / O

4b Underline the key words in the questions above. Match the questions with these extracts from Part 7.

a We were so late I didn't get chance to get out on my surfboard that day – how irritating!
b Situated high in the rainforest canopy, the fascinating tree houses are available all year.
c It was a bit of a let-down as far as learning about another culture was concerned.
d I was so pleased to get home in one piece after so many disasters along the way!
e Frequent delays and cancellations cause holiday-makers a lot of frustration.
f In terms of being 'friendly' towards the local environment, this is one of the best resorts.

5 Read the titles and sub-headings. What kind of information will be included in the texts?

a
HoliBlog
Journalist Heather Ellithorn keeps us up-to-date
as she spends some time in little-known tourist
destination, Comoros.

b
Photographing the wild
Go! magazine's favourite wildlife photographers detail their most
challenging projects in remote areas of the world

c
Into Africa
Georgie Wright tells The Travel Mag about her gap year in Ghana,
volunteering on a children's educational programme.

6 Read the posts. Which of Squid's suggestions do you think would work well for you? Why?

20 comments ▼

mr_nice_guy
How should I tackle Reading, Part 7? Is it better to read the
questions or the texts first? Thanks!
Reply | Like | Posted January 30th at 1.00pm

Squid
The questions come first, so you can read them and think about
them as you read the texts. I actually find it easier to read the
texts first and make sure I understand them before looking at the
questions – whichever works for you is fine!
Reply | Like | Posted February 1st at 10.56am

5 WAYS to SMASH!

Reading & Use of English, Part 7:

understanding detail, opinion and attitude

1 Read **each** section or short text carefully and think about the opinions and details stated in it.

2 Underline the **key words** in the questions and look for the same ideas in the text.

3 **Watch out** for words and phrases in the texts which are similar to those in the questions. You may find similar ideas in several texts but only one text contains the correct answer.

4 Look out for the opinions and attitudes of the writer, or any people referred to in the text. Remember that he / she may not use verbs such as *think* or *believe* to state their opinion, but may use a description instead.

> The trip wasn't as exciting as we'd been led to believe.

5 Each section can be chosen more than once, but you should write only one letter as the answer to each question.

EXAM PRACTICE

1 You are going to read four reviews of travel guides. Scan the texts. Which reviews express
- **mainly positive reviews?**
- **mainly negative reviews?**
- **a balanced view?**

You have **four minutes** to complete the task (one minute per task).

2 Read questions 1–10 and choose from the sections (A–D). The sections may be chosen more than once.

Which review	
says that despite its high price, the book is definitely worth purchasing?	1
suggests that some of the information may not be up-to-date?	2
describes an aspect of the book which makes it visually very appealing?	3
mentions the way in which readers can make up for a missing element in the book?	4
points out that the book fails to consider a significant group of possible readers?	5
highlights the book's tendency to discuss certain topics at length?	6
explains the possible reason for one of the ways the writing is presented?	7
discusses the effect the enthusiastic writing style is likely to have on the reader?	8
mentions the inclusion of a useful feature other guides don't have?	9
says the book is useful for research in advance of travelling?	10

Answer every question. If there are any you aren't sure about, you can go back and check them at the end.

Reviews: Top travel guides

Fasten your seatbelts for Jez Boden's whizz through the coolest travel guides on Earth.

A On the Edge of Adventure

Perfect for use on the spot by the gap-year traveller in Africa who wants to know where to eat, sleep and play on a budget, *On the Edge of Adventure* is full to the brim of handy travellers' tips and knowledge, all presented in a highly-accessible format. Although the book lacks the glossy photographs of its counterparts, the reader gets a real flavour of the countries included, with highly-readable descriptive passages and snippets of information about the history and politics of different regions, as well as cultural traditions and a mini phrasebook of several languages – something often missing in books of this type. The only drawback is its heavy reliance on the anecdotes of those who've walked the streets and beaches mentioned in the guide – are the cafés and hostels they mention still in business now? And the print's tiny – but this is no doubt in order to keep costs down for the money-conscious traveller.

B Hicksy's Guide to Europe

This lightweight volume is ideal for sticking in the top of your rucksack and heading off into the unknown. Despite its slim size, *Hicksy's Guide to Europe* is a surprisingly comprehensive guide to the top tourist destinations of Europe. One glaring fault – to my mind at least – is that it caters only for the mid-price range and upwards in terms of restaurant and accommodation options, leaving those counting their pennies to seek out cheaper alternatives themselves. Having said this, the information included is clearly current, making it more likely to be accurate than some other guides of its type, and is clearly laid-out with sections on food and drink, hotels, sights and customs. *Hicksy's Guide* is far from cheap, but with such a fascinating list of places and sights, you won't find much better than this on the travel guide market.

C Tales from the Americas

This weighty guide to North and South America is not exactly portable, but is a brilliant reference for those planning a trip to the Americas. Beautifully-printed on thick paper and with colourful spreads featuring stunning images of local life, *Tales from the Americas* is a volume more likely to find a permanent place on your bookshelf than a temporary one in your suitcase, but is nevertheless a great starting point from which to plan a trip. Its best feature is its list of current, useful local websites, detailing a wide range of accommodation, sights and services in every village, town and city the guide includes. At times, perhaps, it goes into a bit too much detail about the history and politics of the places mentioned, rather than focussing on the more light-hearted reasons for visiting them, but your money certainly won't be wasted.

D Down Under

Down Under is a great little book for first-timers to Australia and New Zealand, and has everything the day-tripper needs to know for brief stop-off visits on a longer tour of Australasia. Although there aren't many pictures of famous sights – the photographers have homed in on interesting aspects of daily life instead – you do get a sense of the contributors' excitement for the places they write about, passing their passion onto the reader, however casual. There are some highly useful pull-out maps of the big cities and handy hints on getting around on a limited amount of money. The only thing it lacks are prices! Whether this was an oversight, or an intentional desire to help the book stand the test of time isn't clear, but the descriptions of accommodation and eating places give readers at least an idea of whether they're high-end or budget.

WRITING

1 **Look at the pictures on these two pages and make up a brief story about a person in one of them. Discuss these questions in pairs.**

- Where is he / she going? Why?
- What has he / she just done?
- How is he / she feeling?

WRITING FOCUS
how to use tenses in story writing

Exam task
Writing, Part 2 (*First for Schools*): story

2 **Read the posts about the story task. Apart from the past simple what other tenses could you use in a story?**

6 comments ▼

Pollypop2
Quick question about the story on the Writing test! My teacher says I don't use enough different tenses when I write a story. I use the past simple – isn't that right??
Reply | Like | Posted February 20th at 2.00pm

JJ
Yes – past simple is good, Polly, but you need to try some other past tenses too. Check out this sample story and you'll see what I mean.
Reply | Like | Posted February 20th at 2.35pm

3 **Look at the exam task. Now read the story on page 96 and underline one example of each different tense used.**

You have seen this advertisement on an international students' website.

What a story!

Enter our story competition and win a trip to a famous city. Write a story beginning with this sentence:

I'd been looking forward to the trip for ages.

Your story must include:

- an announcement

- a hat

---

4 **Which of the tenses you have underlined …**

a … shows a single, completed action in the past?

b … shows an action in progress in the past?

c … shows a speculation about the past?

d … shows an action that was in progress before a point in the past?

e … shows a future fact?

f … shows an action without an active subject / agent?

g … shows an action that happened before a point in the past?

6 WAYS to SMASH!

Writing, Part 2 (*First for Schools*):

using a range of tenses in a story

1 Use past perfect and past perfect continuous to talk about things that happened before the event you are describing.

> How far had he drifted?

2 Use past continuous to describe what is going on at the time you are talking about.

> I was travelling by ferry.

3 Speculate about what might have happened before, or what you could have done (but didn't).

> There could have been a different ending.

4 Use passive forms when you don't know or don't need to mention the person who did the action.

> The peace was shattered.

5 Use some direct speech, including present, future and present perfect tenses.

> 'The emergency is over,' she said.

6 Use markers to show the sequence of events, e.g. *first, then, after that, at last, finally.*

EXAM PRACTICE

1 **Read the exam task again. Plan and write your own story in 140–190 words. You can use the photographs on these pages as inspiration or think of something completely different. This time the items to include are:**

- an old friend
- a cup of coffee

2 **Share your story with the class and decide whose story should win the competition.**

Right or wrong?

READING

TOPIC
moral issues and crime

READING FOCUS
how to prepare for the
Reading and Use of
English test

Exam task
Reading and Use of English,
Parts 1–7

WRITING FOCUS
how to prepare for and
answer the set text question

Exam task
Writing, Part 2 *(First for
Schools)*: set text

1 Look at the picture. Discuss this question in pairs. Which of these issues
does this picture best illustrate?

- bullying
- marketing
- social pressure

2 Which of the following do you think are, or should be classed as,
crimes? Discuss your ideas in pairs.

- Supermarkets or shops which gain from misleading their customers with
  'bargains' which don't really save you money.
- Peer pressure: pressuring others into doing something which they feel
  uncomfortable with so they don't lose favour among people of their
  own age.
- Bullying people by making comments on their Facebook or other social
  media page where everyone can read them.

*The Reading and Use of English test is 1 hour and 15 minutes long.
There are no time limits for the individual parts of the paper and you
can complete them in any order.*

3 Read Astrid_star's post and write three tips for her.

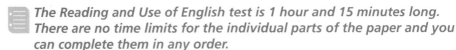

7 comments ▼

Astrid_star
Help! It's my Cambridge First exam tomorrow!! I'm a bit worried
about the Reading test – has anyone got any last-minute advice?
Reply | Like | Posted March 2nd at 2.15pm

4a Work in pairs and answer the questionnaire.

Are you ready ...

for the First Reading and Use of English test? Find out in this quiz!

1 **What's the best advice? Match the advice for Part 1 of the test with the reasons a and b.**

1 Read the whole text first for general understanding.
2 Check whether the word you've chosen fits the context and grammar of the sentence.

a Reading the whole sentence including the option will help you decide whether it 'sounds right'.
b This will definitely help you when it comes to choosing your answers as you'll understand the context better.

2 **Are these statements about Part 2 of the test true or false?**

a You won't be tested on lexical (rather than grammatical) items in this part of the test.   T / F
b You have to complete the gaps in order.   T / F
c You should only write one word for each gap.   T / F
d The words before and after the gap will help you decide which word is missing.   T / F

3 **What kind of changes might you have to make to a word in Part 3? Tick all that apply.**

a adding a prefix
b adding a suffix
c changing a verb to a noun
d changing the form of a verb

4 **Which of the following (a or b) is not a good transformation and why not? Can you improve the unsuccessful transformation?**

a 'Do you know why the burglar alarm didn't go off?' asked the shop owner.   IF
The shop owner asked me what I knew about the burglar alarm didn't go off.

b I'm sure it wasn't Charles Oliver who burgled the property.   HAVE
It can't have been Charles Oliver who burgled the property.

5 **What can go wrong in Part 5? Complete the gaps with words from the box.**

> context | option | instructions | text | words

a Not reading the .... These tells you what you're going to read about and what you have to do.
b Choosing more than one .... Only one is correct!
c Choosing an answer because you've seen one of the .... in the ....
d Not finding out the .... by reading the sentences before and after where you think the answer is.

Are you ready ...

6 Which instruction from Part 6 is not correct? Why?

a There is one extra sentence which you do not need to use.

b Mark your answers on the separate answer sheet.

c Seven sentences have been removed from the article.

d Choose from the sentences A–G the one which fits each gap.

7 What do you think is the best way to approach Part 7 and why? Put the sentences in order.

a Read the questions.

b Write your answer.

c Find similar ideas to the questions in the text.

d Read the text.

e Check whether the section of text and question mean the same.

f Underline key words in the questions.

Remember to mark or write your answers clearly on the separate answer sheet. Answers written on the exam paper will not be marked.

4b Which piece of advice from the questionnaire will help *you* do better in the Reading and Use of English test?

6 WAYS to SMASH!

Reading & Use of English: the test

1 Read **everything** in the test, including the instructions, headings and subheadings.

2 Underline key words in the **questions** where relevant. Refer back to these as you tackle each question.

3 Read all the **options** carefully. Remember not to leap for the first answer which seems right because it contains similar words to the text.

4 If you aren't **sure** about an answer, don't worry. You can go back to it later if you have time.

5 In Parts 5–7, **remember** that the questions will always be in the same order as the text. This will help you to locate the answer.

6 Don't spend too long on an answer you aren't sure about. If in doubt – guess the answer! You won't lose anything, so **give it a go**!

1 Read the text about a criminal and answer questions 1–4.

Real-life criminals: Jack the Ripper

Jack the Ripper was a murderer who killed five or more women in the Whitechapel **(1)** .... of London in 1888. The case was **(2)** .... solved, and the identity of Jack the Ripper remains a mystery. Now a tour of Whitechapel which visits the murder sites is available, where you will find out more about the murders and the suspects of these **(3)** .... crimes.

1 Decide which answer (**A**, **B**, **C** or **D**) best fits the gap.

   A bit   **B** piece   **C** area   **D** section

2 Think of the word which best fits the gap.

3 Use the word **TERROR** to form a word which fits in the gap.

4 Complete the second sentence so that it has a similar meaning to the first using the word given.

   Modern criminal profiling would have enabled the police to identify Jack the Ripper.

   The police .... identify Jack the Ripper by using modern criminal profiling.   **HAVE**

2 Read an extract from a text about internet crime and answer questions 5–7.

What is internet crime?

We've all heard of it, but do you know the full extent of what criminals get up to on the net? Organised crime has filtered into several areas of society – including the internet. **(6)** _____The growth in banking and e-commerce has certainly provided a rich breeding ground for crime.

So what are the criminals up to? Everything, it seems, from phishing (false emails which ask for personal details, such as security information) to key logging – where criminals are able to record what you type. While this may seem frightening, crime agencies devote their time to fighting internet crime, and there's plenty of information to help you stay cyber-safe.

5 Choose the answer (**A, B, C** or **D**) which fits best according to the text.

   The writer believes that

   A security agencies are not doing enough to prevent crimes from happening.

   B the blame for internet crime lies with those who have made it accessible.

   C crime is being reduced by the organisations which are affected by it.

   D people can learn to protect themselves against internet crime.

6 Choose from the sentences (**A** and **B**) the one which fits gap 6.

   A This can have serious consequences for individuals and businesses alike.

   B But who could have predicted results such as these?

7 Answer the question. Choose from the first or second paragraph.

   Which paragraph offers reasons for the increase in internet crime?

WRITING

WRITING FOCUS
how to prepare for and
answer the set text question

Exam task
Writing, Part 2 *(First for Schools)*: set text

1 Work in pairs. Read Sky_boy's post. What questions do you think he was asked?

22 comments ▼

Sky_boy
Yeah, if you know your set text well, then it's a good option! There will be one question in Part 2 so you can choose it if you like, but you don't HAVE to do it! It can be an essay, a review, an article or even an email.
Reply | Like | Posted November 29th at 6.57pm

2 Work in pairs and discuss the questions.

- Can you name a famous fictional detective from your country?
- Can you name a famous fictional UK detective?
- Do you enjoy reading detective fiction? Why / Why not?

3a Here are some exam tasks for the Sherlock Holmes story *A Study in Pink*. Match them with the candidates' answers (a-d) on page 77.

1 This is part of an email you have received from your English friend, Claire.

> I've just finished reading *A Study in Pink* and I can't quite understand how Sherlock solved the case in the end. Can you explain??
> Claire x

Write your **email**.

2 Your English class has just had a discussion about *A Study in Pink*. Now your teacher wants you to write this essay for homework.

Compare the characters of Sherlock Holmes and Dr Watson in *A Study in Pink*.

Write your **essay**.

3 You see this announcement in a book magazine.

> We are looking for articles about unusual partnerships in detective fiction.
> Write an article about the detective partnership in *A Study in Pink* and send it to us. We'll publish the three best articles.

Write your **article**.

4 You see this announcement on an international student website.

> Recommended reads!
> We all love a crime novel! Write a review of a detective novel you've read recently that you enjoyed, saying why you enjoyed it and why you would recommend it to our readers.

Write your **review**.

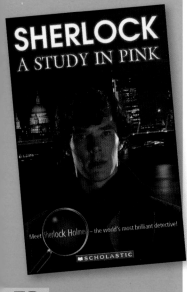

SHERLOCK
A STUDY IN PINK
Meet Sherlock Holmes – the world's most brilliant detective!
SCHOLASTIC

a To begin with, both men are very clever and experienced in their own fields. However, when we look at their personalities, they are worlds apart.

b I had a similar problem so I re-read the final chapter. It's actually very clever! Holmes works out that they were wrong to suspect the passenger of the taxi because ...

c A Study in Pink sees the police baffled again and forced to call on the help of Sherlock Holmes. Several people have died and their deaths look like suicides.

d Two heads are better than one.
At first sight it looks an unlikely combination — an eccentric, violin-playing genius and an ex-army doctor. But it works! How?

3b Read a candidate's answer to one of these questions on page 96. Which question does it answer?

9 WAYS to
SMASH!

Writing, Part 2 (*First for Schools*):

the set text

1 Write short summaries of the **chapters** as you read your set text.

2 Find out some things about the **background** of the book and the writer.

3 Note down some important **vocabulary** while you read each chapter.

4 Think about **themes** in the book, such as friendship or ambition.

5 Write some short descriptions of main **events**.

6 Write some information about the main **characters** and think about **why** you like / don't like them.

7 Think about what makes the **story** interesting and / or exciting.

8 Make sure you **re-read** the text or read your summaries before the test.

9 **Always** answer the question in the test – don't just memorise something you've written before.

The set text changes from time to time. Make sure you've read the right one!

EXAM PRACTICE

1

SMASH! the clock!

Read the exam task. You have 40 minutes to plan your review. Then write your review in 140–190 words.

> Have you read a book recently that you liked a lot?
>
> Write a review of the book for our international website and say why you liked it and why you would recommend it to other readers.

Write your **review**.

2 Read other students' reviews. Which book would you most like to read based on the review? Why?

CAMBRIDGE ENGLISH
Language Assessment
Part of the University of Cambridge

Do not write in this box

Candidate Name
If not already printed, write name
in CAPITALS and complete the
Candidate No. grid (in pencil).

Candidate Signature

Examination Title

Centre

Supervisor:

If the candidate is ABSENT or has WITHDRAWN shade here

Centre No.

Candidate No.

**Examination
Details**

0	0	0	0
1	1	1	1
2	2	2	2
3	3	3	3
4	4	4	4
5	5	5	5
6	6	6	6
7	7	7	7
8	8	8	8
9	9	9	9

Candidate Answer Sheet

Instructions

Use a PENCIL (B or HB).

Rub out any answer you wish
to change using an eraser.

Parts 1, 5, 6 and **7:**
Mark ONE letter for each
question.

For example, if you think **B** is the right
answer to the question, mark your
answer sheet like this:

| 0 | A | B | C | D |

Parts 2, 3 and **4:**
Write your answer clearly
in CAPITAL LETTERS.

For Parts 2 and 3 write one letter
in each box. For example:

| 0 | E X A M P L E |

Part 1

1	A	B	C	D
2	A	B	C	D
3	A	B	C	D
4	A	B	C	D
5	A	B	C	D
6	A	B	C	D
7	A	B	C	D
8	A	B	C	D

Part 2

Do not write
below here

9		9 1 0 u
10		10 1 0 u
11		11 1 0 u
12		12 1 0 u
13		13 1 0 u
14		14 1 0 u
15		15 1 0 u
16		16 1 0 u

Continues over ➡

FCE R

DP802

78

Part 3

		Do not write below here
17		17 1 0 u
18		18 1 0 u
19		19 1 0 u
20		20 1 0 u
21		21 1 0 u
22		22 1 0 u
23		23 1 0 u
24		24 1 0 u

Part 4

		Do not write below here
25		25 2 1 0 u
26		26 2 1 0 u
27		27 2 1 0 u
28		28 2 1 0 u
29		29 2 1 0 u
30		30 2 1 0 u

Part 5

31	A B C D
32	A B C D
33	A B C D
34	A B C D
35	A B C D
36	A B C D

Part 6

37	A B C D E F G
38	A B C D E F G
39	A B C D E F G
40	A B C D E F G
41	A B C D E F G
42	A B C D E F G

Part 7

43	A B C D E F
44	A B C D E F
45	A B C D E F
46	A B C D E F
47	A B C D E F
48	A B C D E F
49	A B C D E F
50	A B C D E F
51	A B C D E F
52	A B C D E F

denote Print Limited 0121 520 5100

Part 1

For questions **1 – 8**, read the text below and decide which answer (**A**, **B**, **C** or **D**) best fits each gap. There is an example at the beginning (**0**).

Mark your answers **on the separate answer sheet**.

Example:

0   **A** watched   **B** remarked   **C** noticed   **D** looked

0	A	B	C	D
	☐	☐	▬	☐

The oldest cave art in the world

More than twenty years ago, climbers in the south of France **(0)** .... air coming through some rocks. They **(1)** .... the small opening and discovered an amazing cave. Chauvet's Cave, as it is now **(2)** .... , is believed to have the oldest cave art in the world. 32,000 years ago people drew pictures that show a **(3)** .... of different wild animals, including bears and lions, on the walls. There are many caves containing primitive art, but these are remarkable **(4)** .... they are clever and precise.

A similar cave in France had been discovered fifty years **(5)** .... this one. Unfortunately, the wonderful art was damaged because so many tourists were **(6)** .... to go inside. It turned **(7)** .... that the change in atmosphere badly affected the paintings. The authorities decided immediately that this would not happen to Chauvet's Cave. Experts have spent four years building an exact copy of the cave with all the drawings for the public. Now visitors can **(8)** .... the beauty of the cave without damaging it.

1	**A** looked	**B** uncovered	**C** studied	**D** investigated
2	**A** considered	**B** known	**C** termed	**D** referred
3	**A** subject	**B** range	**C** choice	**D** history
4	**A** due	**B** according	**C** because	**D** for
5	**A** before	**B** previous	**C** earlier	**D** formerly
6	**A** let	**B** consented	**C** agreed	**D** allowed
7	**A** up	**B** in	**C** over	**D** out
8	**A** like	**B** wonder	**C** appreciate	**D** delight

Part 2

For questions **9 – 16**, read the text below and think of the word which best fits each gap. Use only **one** word in each gap. There is an example at the beginning (**0**).

Write your answers **IN CAPITAL LETTERS on the separate answer sheet**.

Example: | 0 | | W | H | E | R | E |

The Siberian Forest Cat

The Siberian Forest Cat is an ancient breed which originates from Russia, **(0)** .... it is considered the national cat and, as such, **(9)** .... appeared in Russian folk tales and paintings dating back centuries. Widely regarded **(10)** .... one of the largest and most handsome breeds **(11)** .... domesticated cat, the Siberian, as it is more commonly known, has a thick triple coat, which enables the animal to cope **(12)** .... the harsh winter climate of its home territory. **(13)** .... terrific hunter and climber, the Siberian is both athletic and highly energetic, and is as powerfully-built as **(14)** .... is beautiful to look at, with muscular legs and a large barrel-shaped body. Its semi-long hair comes in an impressive range of colours and its full bushy tail is often held up high in greeting. Yet **(15)** .... its size and appearance of great strength, the Siberian is sweet in character, and **(16)** .... known for its tiny 'meow' and loud purr.

Part 3

For questions **17 – 24**, read the text below. Use the word given in capitals at the end of some of the lines to form a word that fits in the gap **in the same line**. There is an example at the beginning (**0**).

Write your answers **IN CAPITAL LETTERS on the separate answer sheet.**

Example: | 0 | | D | E | N | Y | I | N | G |

Healthy honey

Like it or loathe it, there is no **(0)** .... that in terms of both nutrition and	**DENY**
medicine, honey is incredibly **(17)** .... This sweet golden liquid produced	**VALUE**
by bees has been **(18)** .... proven to benefit the whole body. Its antibacterial	**SCIENTIFIC**
properties are well-known, and as raw honey is an **(19)** .... sugar. It remains	**PROCESS**
pure, and is therefore able to provide a quick energy boost when mixed into water	
as a pre-workout drink.	
Not only is honey a **(20)** .... sweetener and a food in itself, but it may also help	**NATURE**
those who experience **(21)** .... allergies to flower particles known as pollen. As	**SEASON**
yet, clinical studies have been unable to prove its **(22)** .... in this area, but the	**EFFECT**
theory is that since honey contains small amounts of pollen, allergy **(23)**	**SUFFER**
who consume small quantities of it over time, may build up antibodies. This results	
in a less **(24)** .... physical response when the person is exposed to pollen.	**DRAMA**

Part 4

For questions **25 – 30**, complete the second sentence so that it has a similar meaning to the first sentence, using the word given. **Do not change the word given**. You must use between **two** and **five** words, including the word given. Here is an example (**0**).

Example:

0 My friend took us to the airport in her car.

  LIFT

  We …………………......................……………… my friend to the airport.

The gap can be filled by the words 'were given a lift by', so you write:

Example: | **0** | WERE GIVEN A LIFT BY

Write **only** the missing words **IN CAPITAL LETTERS on the separate answer sheet**.

---

25 You can't have seen Jo in town – she's on holiday.

  YOU

  It can't have ……………….....................……………… in town – she's on holiday.

26 'I don't know if I'll go to the party or not,' Louisa said.

  GO

  Louisa said that she didn't know ……………….....................……………… to the party or not.

27 We don't seem to have any coffee left.

  OUT

  It looks like ……………….....................……………… of coffee.

28 I regret staying at home all day.

WISH

I ………………...................…................ at home all day.

29 Alessandro says that there aren't any classes today.

NO

There are ………………...................…................ to Alessandro.

30 I'd rather you didn't leave the window open.

MIND

Would ………………...................…................ the window open?

Part 5

You are going to read an article about a form of exercise called yoga. For questions **31 – 36**, choose the answer (**A**, **B**, **C** or **D**) which you think fits best according to the text.

Mark your answers **on the separate answer sheet**.

The power of yoga

It's the end of a long day. You overslept, tackled a tricky project at work, spilled coffee on your shirt and, against your better judgement, engaged in a family drama at home. On top of that, the washing machine leaked all over the kitchen and you burnt your dinner. You're dreading the thought of tomorrow and the possibility of further problems. If only there was the time to squeeze some fitness in as well – a workout that benefits both mind and body.

The solution to feeling better about and dealing with daily challenges might just be found in yoga. This age-old form
line 6 of exercise centres around completing a series of movements which help to develop strength and flexibility. It also focuses on breathing, with the aim of improving physical and mental well-being. 'Yoga activates the parasympathetic nervous system, which is the "relax and chill" part of your brain,' says William J. Broad, author of *The Science of Yoga: The Risks and the Rewards*. When you practise yoga regularly, you learn how to trigger that on your own. 'That way,' says Broad, 'your default reaction to stress becomes "Stay calm!" rather than rushing into panic mode.'

Yoga's not only about relaxing and not worrying about things beyond your control. Holding challenging poses (physical positions) gives you a full-body burn. That means it's great all-round training if you're an athlete and a perfect introduction to fitness if you're amongst the less athletically-inclined. Working a little yoga into your daily routine means you'll get stronger, stretch out your muscles, stand up taller and improve your balance. In other words, it's a win-win situation for everyone. Some also find rewards in working on a challenging pose and eventually mastering it, though even simple poses reap benefits.

Experts recommend attending a series of classes initially in order to ensure you're achieving the correct positions and avoiding injury. Of course, fitting in a trip to the gym after work or college can feel like a chore, especially if you have a home and family to look after or studying to do. But it is certainly a worthwhile investment of your time, because once you've got the basics, you can practise yoga anywhere you like. Take waiting, for example – this is the perfect opportunity to try out what's known as the tree pose, which is essentially standing on one leg. There's no suggestion that you should do this in public where people might stare at you, but there's everything to gain by trying it out when you're hanging around for the microwave to ping or filling the bath. Think of all the time you spend standing around. Why not seize these moments to improve your balance, strengthen your core muscles (great for your posture), and get a good stretch (great for all-over fitness)?

Standing and waiting is not the only time you can use yoga to your advantage. Humans were not meant to sit hunched over a computer screen for hours on end, as many of us are required to do on a daily basis. During breaks, use the time to stretch out your spine, opening up your chest and hips. Not only will you feel a strength-building burn in your legs, but doing back-bending yoga poses can help reverse the damage from too much sitting. And as well as physical conditioning and relaxation, yoga also increases our ability to focus. In a sports science study, thirty people did twenty minutes of yoga, and another thirty ran on a treadmill in the gym for the same amount of time. Afterwards, both groups of people were given cognitive tasks to do and those whose who had done yoga outperformed the others in terms of reaction times and accuracy. So, with all the benefits for body and soul that yoga brings, what are you waiting for?

31 What feeling is captured in the first paragraph?

    A annoyance about having failed to stick to an exercise routine

    B disappointment about having little time to complete household tasks

    C frustration about the difficulties of setting aside time for healthy activities

    D concern about the number of things that need to be achieved in the near future

32 What does 'it' refer to in line 6?

    A breathing

    B strength and flexibility

    C physical and mental well-being

    D an age-old form of exercise

33 The writer includes quotes from William J. Broad to

    A describe how people who do yoga are able to help others in times of need.

    B explain how the brains of those who do yoga differ from those who do not.

    C point out that people who do yoga are able to fight negative feelings without help.

    D support a theory that people who are attracted to yoga regularly suffer from stress.

34 What is the writer doing in the third paragraph?

    A pointing out that yoga can be attempted by people of all abilities

    B encouraging readers to try out more difficult yoga positions

    C suggesting that athletes benefit most from doing yoga

    D recommending that yoga is done as a warm-up for other sports

35 What opinion does the writer express about doing yoga in the fourth paragraph?

    A It is important to take advice from yoga specialists.

    B People may find it embarrassing to adopt certain yoga practices.

    C People prefer to get everyday tasks done than make time for yoga.

    D It can be challenging for people to find the time to do yoga properly.

36 How does the writer conclude the article in the final paragraph?

    A by describing the long-term benefits of regular yoga practice

    B by providing additional support for arguments in favour of yoga

    C by acknowledging that further research into the usefulness of yoga is required

    D by suggesting that there is little point engaging in certain other forms of exercise

Part 6

You are going to read a magazine article about American Yearbooks. Six sentences have been removed from the article. Choose from the sentences **A – G** the one which fits each gap (**37 – 42**). There is one extra sentence which you do not need to use.

Mark your answers **on the separate answer sheet**.

Is it the end of the American Yearbook?

It's graduation day. High school students all over the US are saying their final farewells as they prepare to walk out of the school gates for one last time. With them they'll have a memento of their year – their yearbook, a record of their final year and achievements at school. Or will they?

The yearbook is an American institution. Written and produced by students in their final year, a yearbook contains the photos and messages of students as well as the memories and highlights of the school year, including sports results, drama productions and school vacations. Twenty-year-old Gabriel from Chicago is flicking through: 'I often look back at my yearbook and think of the great memories I had ... and I love seeing how myself and my classmates have changed!' Alicia agrees: 'I love looking back at my yearbooks. It always makes me smile. I feel just like the teenager I was at the time. It's also getting funnier as I get older to look at the clothes and the hairstyles!' The yearbook serves to remind people of all the good times they had at school and what they achieved. | **37** |

Students and high schools invest serious time and money in the books. There are yearbook editorial teams and a teacher who takes charge of the production. | **38** | Alicia, who now works in publishing, says: 'I was on the yearbook staff in high school and learned many skills including layout, editing, budgeting, photography and teamwork.' It is excellent preparation for a career in journalism.

And then there's the all important photos. Students splash out on new clothes, a particular item of jewellery or get their hair done to look their best. | **39** | 'There's a lot of pressure to look good,' says Gabriel. 'Who wants to look back at their photo and feel embarrassed?'

But Gabriel and Alicia's yearbooks may become a tradition of the past. As school budgets are cut, it's hard for schools to justify spending thousands of dollars on printing the complex books. Many schools are looking for cheaper solutions such as digital yearbooks – and some schools no longer publish the books at all. | **40** | High schools report fewer and fewer sales year on year.

| **41** | Social media sites mean that students can easily relive or share their school memories by going online. One yearbook printer admits interest in yearbooks has waned. He believes that it is not that students aren't interested, but that Facebook and other social networking opportunities offer more readily available and attractive venues than the old yearbook world.

Gabriel disagrees. 'I don't think that social media could ever replace a yearbook. It's the one thing students from the digital age want a hard copy of.' Perhaps she's right. Yearbooks are like time capsules. | **42** | It may be nostalgic, it may collect dust on a shelf but it will still be there in the future to look though and bring back memories.

A Unlike digital records of our lives which can be continually updated, the yearbook is an item that will never change and reflects an important time in our youth.

B This whole process can take ages as students think carefully about what they want to include on their page, which quotes should accompany their photos and so on.

C There's another threat to the traditional high school yearbook.

D However, a lot of teenagers see them as old-fashioned and fewer are interested in helping to produce them today.

E At a time when students are trying to save money, the cost of buying a yearbook is also an expensive luxury that many are beginning to cut down on.

F In addition to this, it recalls forgotten friendships and the important teachers who had an impact on their lives.

G This can cost them, or their parents, a lot of money.

Part 7

You are going to read a magazine article reviewing four books. For questions **43 – 52**, choose from the sections (**A – D**). The sections may be chosen more than once.

Mark your answers **on the separate answer sheet**.

Which book

leads the reader to doubt the narrator's story?	**43**	
uses the natural environment to affect the development of the story?	**44**	
refers to events in another book?	**45**	
can provoke different reactions in the same reader?	**46**	
has more than one narrator?	**47**	
has a location which restricts action?	**48**	
deals with some philosophical questions about writers and writing?	**49**	
was not bought by the reviewer herself?	**50**	
is one of a large number written by a prolific writer?	**51**	
has an unanticipated ending?	**52**	

Book Choice

Karen Smith writes about her favourite recent reads.

A One of my favourite books of the last few years has to be *Elizabeth is Missing* by Emma Healey. A friend lent me his copy a few months ago and having read the blurb on the back, I was intrigued. How could someone write a mystery story from the point of view of an old lady with dementia? This seeming impossibility encouraged me to start reading and I was immediately hooked. It was one of the cleverest books I've ever read and I was captivated by the way the main character finds her way through her poor memory to discover why her friend Elizabeth is missing. The storyline unfolds as pieces of the puzzle fall into place but it never becomes over-complicated or confusing. There are some very moving moments but also some hilarious ones. Emma Healey studied Creative Writing at my old university, so I had an added interest in reading the book.

B One of the most popular books last year was *The Ice Twins* by S. K. Tremayne. It's a psychological thriller and is mainly set on an isolated Scottish island. It deals with the story of the aftermath of the death of a twin and follows the lives of the surviving twin and the parents over the following year. One reason that I particularly enjoyed it was because the story is told from two points of view – that of the mother and that of the father. Obviously they see, interpret and remember things in different ways and the reader is kept guessing about what really happened until the final surprising climax. The desolate location is beautifully described and that, together with the build-up of a terrifying storm, contributes to the frightening events that the family experience.

C I simply can't get enough of Stephen King and it seems that a lot of people feel the same way. *Finders Keepers*, a recent novel in the *Mr Mercedes* series, is no disappointment to his enormous number of fans and is guaranteed to keep you up reading until the small hours. The story focuses on several characters who, in the previous novel, were involved in a disaster at a job fair where hundreds of people queuing to apply for jobs were killed or injured. The book also considers the value of modern novels in both literary and social terms. Well-written, as always, the pace of King's writing maintains a high state of tension throughout and I'm sure it has brought the legendary writer many new readers as well as great satisfaction to the ones who have followed his nightmarish journeys over the past few decades.

D *Little Girl Gone* was a runaway bestseller when it was first released and it isn't difficult to see why. It concerns the disappearance of a young baby and the focus of the police on the traumatised mother as a suspect for the child's murder. What is striking about this book is that it's told by the mother who is insistent that she has no memory of what happened. She is being helped by a psychotherapist to recall the events and most of the story is told while she is in an institution. The reader is never sure how much she is revealing or how much she is hiding which keeps us interested. There is actually very little physical action until the last few chapters but the unfolding narrative and the way in which events are recalled is spellbinding and it never loses pace. Alexandra Burt is a talented writer and I can't wait to see what her next novel will be about.

9 ways to SMASH! Writing:

the test

1 Think about the person who is going to read what you write. Decide whether your style should be formal or informal.

2 Plan your answer carefully and make notes before you start.

3 Organise your work well and divide your answer into clear and logical paragraphs. Think carefully about the opening and closing paragraphs – introduce your topic well and conclude appropriately.

4 Use discourse markers to guide the reader through your writing easily. Use linking words to combine ideas within or across sentences.

5 Vary your sentence length to provide interest. Use a range of vocabulary and structures to show your skills.

6 Engage the reader with direct questions and a thought-provoking or amusing ending.

7 Make sure you have included everything the question asks for.

8 Always check your work for spelling, punctuation and grammatical mistakes.

9 Put yourself in the role of the reader and ask yourself if you are fully informed.w

WRITING PRACTICE TEST

Part 1

You **must** answer this question. Write your answer in **140 – 190** words in an appropriate style on the separate answer sheet.

1 In your English class you have been talking about advertising. Now, your English teacher has asked you to write an essay.

Write an essay using **all** the notes and giving reasons for your point of view.

> Some people say that advertising has a bad effect on people's lives. Do you agree?
>
> **Notes**
>
> Write about:
>
> 1. information
>
> 2. buying unnecessary things
>
> 3. .... (your own idea)

Part 2

Write an answer to **one** of the questions **2 – 4** in this part. Write your answer in **140 – 190** words in an appropriate style on the separate answer sheet. Put the question number in the box at the top of the answer sheet.

---

2   You see this announcement on an English-language website.

> ### Articles wanted
>
> What's changed in your area recently? Has it changed for the better or for the worse?
>
> Write an article about it and we'll put the best on the website.

Write your **article**

3   You have received this email from your English-speaking friend Mark.

> **From:** Mark
>
> **Subject:** Sports
>
> I'm doing a project about sports in different countries. I'm writing about sports that people play and those which are popular to watch.
>
> Could you tell me what's traditionally popular in your country? Do lots of people go to see these sports? Can you watch them on TV too?
>
> Thanks,
>
> Mark

Write your **email.**

4   You have seen this announcement on an international website.

> ### Story Competition
>
> Would you like to win some books in our story competition?
>
> Your story must begin with the sentence:
>
> *No one had seen Andy for three days and I was starting to get worried.*
>
> Your story must include:
>
> • a phone
> • a newspaper headline

Write your **story**.

WRITING RESOURCE BANK

1 Big dreams

3b (page 10)

It takes a lot of hard work to get to the top, whether as a sportsperson, in entertainment or in business. But I think that it must be even harder to stay there.

To start with, everyone expects great things from you once you're at the top, whereas when you're on the way up, that's not the case. Now you have to keep coming up with winning performances or tremendous ideas and the pressure must be enormous.

The important question is also how much you want it. Once you've achieved your goal and beaten all the obstacles and competition, you need to find the motivation to keep going. In my opinion that's quite a different skill.

Finally, the person at the top is now the person for others to beat There will always be newer competitors with the same hunger that you used to have. It's hard to keep on winning.

To conclude, I think staying at the top requires a different attitude than it took to get there. Those who are both determined and talented will do it. But they definitely have to watch out for those on their way up!

3 Looking good?

 (page 23)

Dear Alice,

I am writing in response to the advertisement you posted on your website last week for a fashion blogger.

I am a student in my third year of a course in Fashion Journalism at Marley College. I have always been extremely interested in fashion trends and how and why they change. I have designed my own clothes and helped organise fashion shows at college and before that, at school. I have also researched several projects about the history of fashion and I have a particular interest in fifties and sixties design.

Last year I wrote a weekly article for our local free newspaper and I believe that I learned a great deal from the experience.

If you consider me a suitable candidate, please send an application form to lucyparks@marley.ac.com

I look forward to hearing from you,

Yours

Lucy Parks

4 Under pressure

 (page 28)

A

Believe in yourself!

So what's the biggest decision most of us have to make in our lives? I guess that has to be our careers. Think about it. We spend a lot of our lives at work – so it's important to make the right decisions. But that's easier said than done.

We can get all the advice in the world but in the end it comes down to us. And we don't always get it right. I didn't. I studied law at university but I soon realised that I wasn't cut out to be a lawyer. I nearly had a heart attack imagining myself standing up in front of a judge! I had made a big mistake.

My parents weren't sympathetic nor were my lecturers. The pressure to simply carry on was huge. But I knew that it wasn't right for me.

Finally I decided to give up the course. I decided to do something completely different. I went to art school for two years and now I do illustrations for children's books. I love my work. What a good decision that was! It goes to show how important it can be to follow your instincts. Believe in yourself!

B

My most difficult decision

It is very important to choose the correct career. I was a good student and my teachers and parents advised me to study law at university and become a lawyer. Lawyers have a good job and earn a lot of money. I followed their advice and went to university to study law.

However, I soon realised that I didn't want to be a lawyer and I didn't want to continue my course. I spoke to my parents and teachers and they all recommended that I stay at university. They tried very hard to persuade me. They thought I would be a good lawyer and that a university education was very important. I didn't agree with them and I decided to leave university at the end of that term.

After leaving university, I applied to go to art school because I had always enjoyed drawing. When I completed my course, I got some jobs illustrating children's books. I now work regularly and I've become quite successful. I enjoy my work as an illustrator and I'm glad I made the decision to stop studying law.

5 New words for old

 (page 34)

Motivation is key to successful language learning. If you're in another country and you need to be understood, then that is a very strong motivation! However, the motivation to pass exams at school is also strong and can encourage students to continue language learning (and to visit other countries) after they finish their exams.

Some people live for a while in other countries and this is a perfect opportunity to learn the language. But for the majority of people this sort of opportunity is rare and learning at school is the best alternative. It's also true to say that the teaching which students get at school from good language teachers is invaluable.

9 Hardwired to stereotype?

 (page 58)

A friend for life

Just ask anyone today and they'll say they've got lots of friends, sometimes hundreds! But are we undervaluing the word 'friend'? In my opinion, the people we call 'friends'- on social media for example aren't real 'friends'. They are people we know or just acquaintances. That's different.

In my opinion a real friend is someone like my mate Lorrie who I've known since we started school together, aged five. Although we're the same age, we're very different in many other ways. For example, we come from different backgrounds. My parents are teachers whereas Lorrie's are politicians. I'm into books and I'm studying Literature at university whereas Lorrie loves sports and is studying Sports Psychology.

The basis of a good friendship in my opinion is firstly to be supportive and secondly to have similar attitudes to important things. For example, Lorrie's opinions about what's right or wrong and her attitudes to things like celebrity culture are similar to mine. Although we sometimes disagree, we are still friends afterwards.

I know that Lorrie and I will truly be friends for life. You can't say that about many people, can you?

11 Travellers' tales

 (page 70)

I'd been looking forward to the trip for ages. I was travelling by ferry across the English Channel to stay with my French friend. I found a seat next to a porthole and watched the sun setting over the calm sea.

Then suddenly the peace was shattered. Someone screamed, 'Help! There's a person in the water!'
Men in yellow jackets rushed to the deck and the big ferry slowly stopped. Everyone was worried about the poor person in the water. Could he swim? How far had he drifted?

After about fifteen minutes there was an announcement. 'The emergency is over,' a lady with a French accent said. 'It was a mistake. No one fell into the water. It was only a hat! It fell from a passenger's head as he was looking at the sea. The ferry will now continue its journey. Please be careful when you are on the deck!'

All the passengers laughed and the boat started to move again. No one was hurt and that was a relief. But there could have been a different ending. I certainly didn't go on deck for the rest of the journey!

12 Right or wrong?

 (page 77)

Everyone has heard of the wonderfully eccentric detective Sherlock Holmes, and the book 'A Study in Pink' shows him at the very top of his game! It's about a case that follows the first meeting of Sherlock and his famous partner Dr Watson and it was so good that I read the whole book in one evening.

'A Study in Pink' sees the police baffled and forced to call on the help of Sherlock Holmes. Several people have died and their deaths look like suicides. But are they? Sherlock uses his amazingly sharp, logical mind to find the unexpected answer. Dr Watson proves very useful too – at one point saving the detective's life!

In my opinion, this book has everything you want in good detective fiction. There is an exceptionally clever plot and the main characters are unusual and likeable. Sherlock's clever deductions really make us think and the action is fast-moving and keeps our attention.

For anyone who doesn't know Sherlock Holmes, this book is a great introduction. For those who know and love him, it's a brilliant example of his skills! Go out and buy it!

Unit 1

Reading

1   Students' answers

2a They are all non-fiction except for a novel.

 b Students' answers

3–4 Students' answers

5a **1** c **2** d **3** b **4** a

 b **a** predicting the information the text might contain and reading the instructions for detail   **b** predicting   **c** skimming   **d** reading for detail   **e** scanning   **f** scanning   **g** reading for detail

6   Students' answers

EXAM PRACTICE

1a & b Students' answers

2a a Jade's ambition is to represent her country as a professional swimmer. **b** Her professional life coach, Ailish Campbell, is going to help her achieve it. **c** Missy Franklin is her favourite sportsperson.

 b D

Writing

1a & b Students' answers.

2   Students' answers. Photos (clockwise, from left): Taylor Swift (singer-songwriter); Mark Zuckerberg (Facebook entrepreneur); Lewis Hamilton (Formula 1 racing driver)

3a & b Students' answers

4   **a** *It takes a lot of hard work to get to the top, whether as a sportsperson, in entertainment or in business.*
   b *To conclude*   **c** *it takes a lot; whether; it must be even harder; whereas; you have to keep coming up with; once you've achieved; you need to find; there will always be; you used to have; staying at the top requires*

EXAM PRACTICE

1a & b Students' answers

Unit 2

Reading

1   Students' answers. The sitcoms in the photographs are: (clockwise, from left): *Friends; How I Met Your Mother; The Big Bang Theory.*

2a **Part 1** answering a multiple-choice question
   Part 2 writing a missing word   **Part 3** writing the correct form of a word to fill a gap   **Part 4** re-writing part of a sentence

 b Part 1 involved   **Part 2** of   **Part 3** viewers
   Part 4 was watched by 20-somethings who

3a Students' answers

 b Part 5 answering a multiple-choice question
   Part 6 completing a text with a missing sentence
   Part 7 matching a text and question

 c a 6   **b** 5   **c** 7

EXAM PRACTICE

1a Students' answers

 b Part 6 **1** B
   Part 7 **1** C   **2** B   **3** A

Writing

1   Students' answers

2a You need to incorporate the first sentence which has been provided, and the two things given as prompts.

 b Students' answers

3   **a** The writer answers all the questions except where the water came from.   **b** Yes, it is. The story is divided into clear paragraphs. The writer sets the scene at the beginning and there is a positive ending.   **c** The dialogue makes the story more interesting.

4   **a** deafening   **b** very nervous / terrified   **c** brilliant / wonderful / great   **d** completely silent

5   Suggested answers: **a** exhausted / worn out   **b** furious / mad   **c** ecstatic / elated / thrilled   **d** freezing / icy   **e** terrible / appalling / awful / dreadful / horrid   **f** huge / enormous / giant / gigantic / massive   **g** packed / full   **h** tiny / microscopic / minute   **i** filthy   **j** hilarious

6   Students' answers

EXAM PRACTICE

1–3 Students' answers

Unit 3

Reading

1–3 Students' answers

4   Suggested answers: **a** Luke wanted to get more muscular quickly because his exercising routine wasn't helping much but the protein shakes he started taking made him ill.   **b** A   **c** no

5   **a** be aware and a bit ashamed of how you look   **b** get more muscle   **c** when all the muscles in your abdomen are well-developed   **d** a drink containing added protein

e looking for f physical appearance g natural for people h increased the number of i (He) got what (he) wanted but there were disadvantages to it. j arms and legs

EXAM PRACTICE

1 **1** B **2** C **3** D **4** C

2–3 Students' answers

Writing

1 Students' answers

2 **a** to ask for information on a course **b** no **c** They're too colloquial and informal. These phrases are more appropriate for an email to a friend. **d** Students' answers

3

	Informal emails	More formal emails
1	Hello Amy	Dear Mr Browne
2	I thought I'd drop you a line to say …	–
3	Love, J	Yours faithfully, Yours sincerely
4	it's, I'd	They are, it is, I would
5	Sounds great!	I was surprised to hear your news.
6	because of this	therefore

4 Suggested answers:

A: Email. Informal language: *Hi Eva, / How's it going? / I need your help! / It would be great if / trending / Which looks are hot right now and who's cool? / your mates / Love, Charlie x*

B: Online job advertisement. Formal language: *vacancy / has arisen / The successful candidate / will relate directly to / with a background in / please contact / suitable for the position*

5 Suggested answers: *Dear Alice, / I am writing in response to / I have always been extremely interested in / I have a particular interest in / I believe that I learned a great deal / If you consider me a suitable candidate, please send an application form to / I look forward to hearing from you / Yours, Lucy Parks*

EXAM PRACTICE

1 Students' answers

2 Hi Charlie,

Thanks for your email. Great to hear from you as always! Sounds an interesting project. You're actually asking the right person because I LOVE fashion and I'm always out buying clothes!

Right now, a lot of new styles are trending. Hats are very big (!) for girls and guys and some eighties-style clothes are making a comeback. There's a trend here at the moment to wear something tartan with an outfit – maybe just on the edge of a pocket?

Most of the kids I know copy the look of a singer or celebrity they like. Crazy really, as they sometimes look very weird! Of course, kids with money want to have all the latest designer clothes – even though they end up looking just the same as each other!! As for me, I know what I like and what suits me, so I tend to develop my own style.

Hope that helps!

Eva x

3 Students' answers

Unit 4

Reading

1 Students' answers

2 **a** lose **b** get **c** keep **d** burst

3 **1** c **2** b **3** a

4 **a** stay calm **b** the heat is on **c** took up

5 **1** a **2** b **3** b

6a Students' answers

b adjective: anxious, cool, irritated, nervous, stress-free; phrasal verb: calm down, chill out; stress someone out; noun / verb phrase: be in a panic, be under stress, can't relax

c positive: cool, stress-free, calm down, chill out; negative: anxious, irritated, nervous, stress someone out, be in a panic, be under stress, can't relax

EXAM PRACTICE

1 The article is about how to gain more self-control.

2 Students' answers

3 **1** A **2** C **3** A **4** D **5** B **6** C **7** D **8** B

4 Students' answers

Writing

1–2 Students' answers

3a A

b Suggested answers:

1 Catchy title: *Believe in yourself!*

2 Talk directly to reader, e.g. *So what's …? / Think about it.*

3 Short sentences, e.g. *I didn't.*

4 Strong adjectives, e.g. *huge*

5 Humour, e.g. *I nearly had a heart attack …*

6 Exclamation marks, e.g. *What a good decision that was!*

7 Idioms / colloquial language, e.g. *easier said than done, it comes down to …*

8 Interesting ending: *Believe in yourself.*

4 **a** But that's easier said than done. **b** In the end, it comes down to us. **c** get it right **d** I was not cut out to be … **e** carry on **f** give up **g** It goes to show how … **h** follow your instincts

5 Students' answers

EXAM PRACTICE

1–3 Students' answers

Unit 5

Reading

1–2 Students' answers. Common differences between British English and American English are different spellings, such as *-ise* (BrE) versus *-ize* (AmE) and different words for the same thing (e.g. *chips* versus *fries*).

3 the influence of US culture, new conventions and innovations, the influence of social media

4 **a** *the* – article **b** *dying out* – phrasal verb **c** *but* – conjunction **d** *one* – determiner **e** *may* – modal verb **f** *has* – auxiliary verb **g** *which* – relative pronoun **h** *then* – adverb **i** *it* – pronoun **j** *on* – preposition

5a Students' answers

b a fallen out of fashion **b** no exception **c** replaced by / with

EXAM PRACTICE

1–2 Students' answers

3 **1** will / can **2** being **3** of **4** it **5** the **6** Some **7** which **8** when / once

Writing

1 Students' answers

2a Students' answers. The picture on the top left is from 'la tomatina' – a festival held every year in the east of Spain, where festival-goers throw tomatoes.

b Students' answers

3–4 Students' answers

5 Introduction: A is better because it is engaging, gives a fact and an opinion and asks a question. B is short, simple and boring. Conclusion: B is better because it doesn't repeat everything from the previous paragraphs and finishes on an interesting note. A is not a good conclusion because it relists points already made.

6 **a** can, case **b** On, say **c** summarise, fair, depends **d** in spite of, reasons **e** conclude, clear

EXAM PRACTICE

1–2 Students' answers

Unit 6

Reading

1 Students' answers. The people in the photos are Einstein (physicist), Suzanne Collins (writer of *The Hunger Games* trilogy) and Steve Jobs (co-founder of Apple). A 'lightbulb moment' means a moment of sudden inspiration or realisation.

2 Student's answers

3a **a** invention **b** revolutionised **c** existence **d** popularity **e** industrial **f** communicate **g** incredibly **h** unable

b a noun **b** verb **c** noun **d** noun **e** adjective **f** verb **g** adverb **h** adjective

4 **a** prefixes **b** adjective endings **c** verb endings **d** adverb endings **e** noun endings

5 Student's answers

EXAM PRACTICE

1 attending **2** dropped **3** replays **4** unpleasant **5** improvements **6** technologically **7** generation **8** speech

Writing

1–3 Students' answers

4 He has addressed points 2, 3, 4 and 5 in the *Smash It!* list. But he hasn't answered the question – he's written about a scientist from Alfie's country, not his own.

5 Referring to previous email: *That sounds like a cool project!*

Giving advice and making suggestions: *I think you should include him. / If you go online, you can probably find it.*

Closing an email: *I hope that's helped. / Send me a copy …*

EXAM PRACTICE

1–2 Students' answers

Unit 7

Reading

1–2 Students' answers

3a Students' answers

b a Skyscrapers and boats come to mind. **b** The views from the mountains take my breath away. **c** Some tourists who visit (really) get on my nerves.

4a Students' answers

b a 1 **b** 6 **c** 2 **d** 4 **e** 5 **f** 3

EXAM PRACTICE

1 associate the temples | with   **2** were you | I'd / I would
3 to take | me OR that she would | take me
4 was apparently | made by   **5** you | won't / will not spend
6 is / 's not | as flat as

Writing

1–2 Students' answers

3 **a** Students' answers **b** Yes. Each paragraph deals with a separate point in the task and it makes the essay clear to read.

4a Students' answers

b Many people think that living in an urban environment is better than living somewhere quieter <u>but</u> is that necessarily true?

Pollution can be a problem for your health. Constant traffic produces quite severe air pollution <u>which</u> is not good for us. <u>In addition to this</u>, traffic can cause a lot of noise pollution, <u>although</u> it is not the only cause. Crowds of people and noisy neighbours can <u>also</u> be disruptive.

<u>Another important point is</u> cost. Sometimes the price of accommodation in urban areas can be prohibitive, <u>whereas</u> the same money could get a bigger property in the countryside.

<u>A good point about</u> living in built-up areas <u>is</u> the convenience. Journeys to work are shorter and <u>therefore</u> it's easy to get to theatres, shops and other amenities. There's often a lively, exciting atmosphere <u>which</u> many people like.

To conclude, I must say that much depends on the area, <u>as well as</u> on people's personalities. <u>However</u>, I have to admit that for me the negative points of life in an urban environment definitely outweigh the positive ones. I enjoy the peace and quiet of a rural location.

c Adding: *In addition to this, also, Another important point, A good point about … is …, as well as*
Contrasting: *although, whereas, However*
Giving cause and result: *therefore*
Using relative pronouns: *which*

5 Suggested answers: **a** where people can walk round without needing to look out for traffic. **b** Despite the small garden, my sister and I had loads of fun climbing the one tree. **c** As a result, I made friends in lots of different areas. **d** which has a range of great shops. **e** although I like to go for trips there. **f** whereas I just love noisy, lively places.

EXAM PRACTICE

1–3 Students' answers

Unit 8

Reading

1 Students' answers. The people in the pictures are: (left) taking part in the ice bucket challenge; (centre) taking a selfie with his dog; (right) Beyoncé is taking part in a challenge to take a selfie of herself with no make-up on.

2 Students' answers.

3a The correct answer is B.

A is incorrect because there is no mention of Toby encouraging other people to do the challenge. He mentions his girlfriend, but she helped him complete his challenge, not her own.

C is incorrect because there is no mention of regret in the text. We know Toby gave 'a bit more money' to the charity, but we don't know how much. He seems pleased to have given money, however much that was.

D is incorrect because Toby says that he isn't sure he will repeat the experience any time soon, which suggests that he didn't particularly enjoy it, even though it was worthwhile.

b The part of the text that gives the answer is: *everyone was a winner – how cool is that?*

EXAM PRACTICE

1 **1** b **2** a **3** c

2a **1** B **2** C **3** D

b 1 *'What is wrong with quietly giving money to charity?' asked journalist Michael Wilkinson.*

2 *In fact, only half of those taking the ice bucket challenge mentioned the name of the charity in their videos. Many people seemed more interested in getting 'likes' and comments on their posts than helping the charities.*

3 *'… knowing that more people now know about this disease; my heart is just overwhelmed,' he said.*

The article doesn't use the same words: paraphrases are used to create the same meaning.

3 Students' answers

Writing

1–2 Students' answers

3 **1** Suggested answers: Headings: *Introduction / College run / Computer skills / Sponsored litter clean-up / Conclusion* **2** Introduction: *The purpose of this report is to … and to recommend …* **3** Conclusion: *I would definitely recommend that …* **4** There are no informal phrases. **5** Passive verb forms: *was also raised / were invited* **6** Advanced structures: *Not only did it …*
7 Facts and details: *On 25th May …*

4a **a** definitely   **b** should   **c** idea   **d** would   **e** suggest
   f recommendation

b Students' answers

1–3 Students' answers

Unit 9

Reading

1 Students' answers

2a Students' answers

   b c (the writer offers a balanced view of stereotyping)

   c b and c

3 They are all used as pronouns in this text.

4 **1** c   **2** b   **3** a

5 Paragraph 6: *And we stereotype others not just on their appearance, how they dress or act, but – wrongly – on their race and sex too.*

   Paragraph 7: *But it's too simple to make assumptions that 'they'– teenagers in other groups – are both more alike than they really are, and more different than they are from 'us'. It's easy to throw a group of people into a bucket and judge them as a whole; it's much more difficult to look at each person as an individual.*

EXAM PRACTICE

1 **a** 4   **b** 2 & 3   **c** 1

2 Students' answers

3 **1** C   **2** B   **3** D   **4** C

4 Students' answers

1–2b Students' answers

3 **a** *For instance*, Lorrie's *views* about what's right and wrong and her *thoughts about issues* like celebrity culture and so on are *close to* mine.

   b The basis of a good friendship *for me* is firstly to be supportive.

   c In my opinion a *true* friend is someone like my mate Lorrie.

   d I'm into books and I'm studying Literature *while* Lorrie loves sports and is *doing* Sports Psychology.

   e We sometimes disagree *but* we are still friends afterwards.

4 **a** kind / great / lovely   **b** received   **c** delicious / cool / enjoyable   **d** enjoy   **e** really / extremely   **f** terrible / cold and rainy   **g** a large number of / loads of / many   **h** important / significant

5 Suggested answers: **a** Lorrie loves sports   **b** I'm studying   **c** who I've known   **d** since we started school   **e** Lorrie and I will truly be friends for life

1–2 Students' answers

Unit 10

Reading

1–2 Students' answers

3a b

   b The word 'instead' indicates a contrast, and is followed by what Julianne is actually doing now. The paragraph as a whole focuses on what Julianne is doing.

4a **1** an action   **2** a reason   **3** a feeling

   b Suggested answers: **1** She decides to do some online shopping.   **2** She's got a problem she wants to talk about.   **3** She's really worried when she wakes up.

EXAM PRACTICE

1 **1** B   **2** G   **3** A   **4** D   **5** F   **6** C

2 Students' answers

1–2 Students' answers

3 Suggested answers: **1** name / basic information / summary / opinion   **2** Did you see it?   **3** talented / dramatic   **4** slowly / extremely / particularly   **5** I was hooked … / I loved it!   **6** introduction / summary / opinion

4 **a** and **d**
   b is too short and abrupt and contradicts the rest of the review; **c** contradicts the rest of the review and the focus of the drama is not communication technology

5a Students' answers

   b Suggested answers: **a** absolutely brilliant   **b** exceptionally talented   **c** unintentionally cruel   **d** dramatic climax   **e** superb performance   **f** compulsive viewing

1–2 Students' answers

Unit 11

Reading

1 Students' answers

2 **1** c   **2** e   **3** b   **4** a   **5** d

3   *anxious, doubtful* and *amused* describe how someone is feeling (adjectives). The other words are verb forms: *attempted* = tried, *discovered* = found, *appreciates* = understand how good someone or something is, *emphasises* = highlights, *values* = to consider important

4a **1** O **2** D **3** O **4** D **5** D **6** O

 b **1** c **2** f **3** d **4** b **5** e **6** a

5   Suggested answers: **a** details about the country, its culture and history, as well as things she's been doing and what she plans to see next **b** details about where they went, the challenges they faced and how they solved them **c** details about the programme, what she did and her feelings looking back on it

6   Students' answers

EXAM PRACTICE

1   Students' answers

2   **1** B **2** A **3** C **4** D **5** B **6** C **7** A **8** D **9** A
    10 C

Writing

1–2 Students' answers

3   Suggested answers: I'd been looking forward (past perfect continuous); I was travelling (past continuous); I found a seat, Could he swim? (past simple); The peace was shattered (past passive); How far had he drifted? (past perfect); The emergency is over (present simple); The ferry will now continue. (will for future use); Please be careful (imperative form); There could have been a different ending. (past speculation)

4   **a** Students' answers **b** Students' answers **c** there could have been **d** I'd been looking forward **e** The ferry will now continue **f** the peace was shattered **g** How far had he drifted?

EXAM PRACTICE

1–2 Students' answers

Unit 12

Reading

1–3   Students' answers

4a **1** **1** b **2** a

   2 **a** F **b** F **c** T **d** T

   3 All of these are possible.

   4 **b** is a good transformation. **a** is not a good transformation because it does not accurately reflect what is said in the first sentence (it does not address 'why') , it does not use the target word 'if', and it is not grammatically correct. The correct answer should read: *The shop owner asked me if I knew why the burglar alarm didn't go off.*

5   **a** instructions **b** option **c** words, text **d** context

6   **c** Six sentences have been removed from the article (not seven).

7   **a** 1 or 2 **b** 6 **c** 4 **d** 1 or 2 **e** 5 **f** 3

 b Students' answers

EXAM PRACTICE

1   **1** C **2** never / not **3** terrible **4** would have been able to

2   **5** D **6** A **7** the first paragraph

Writing

1   Suggested answers: Is it a good idea to do the task on the set text? What is the task like?

2   Students' answers

3a **1** b **2** a **3** d **4** c

 b 4

EXAM PRACTICE

1–2 Students' answers

Reading & Use of English Practice Test

Part 1

1 D **2** B **3** B **4** C **5** A **6** D **7** D **8** C

Part 2

9 has **10** as **11** of **12** with **13** A **14** it
15 despite **16** is

Part 3

17 valuable **18** scientifically **19** unprocessed
20 natural **21** seasonal **22** effectiveness **23** sufferers
24 dramatic

Part 4

25 been Jo | (that) you saw **26** whether / if she | would / 'd go **27** we have / 've | run out **28** wish I | had not / hadn't stayed **29** no classes today | according **30** you mind | not leaving

Part 5

31 C **32** D **33** C **34** A **35** D **36** B

Part 6

37 F **38** B **39** G **40** E **41** C **42** A

Part 7

43 D **44** B **45** C **46** A **47** B **48** D **49** C **50** A
51 C **52** B

Writing Practice Test

Sample answers:

1 Essay

Advertising is a big part of our lives today. We see advertisements everywhere we go and whatever we're doing. They're on trains and in the street, on our phones and computers, even on our clothes. It's impossible to escape them! But are these adverts making our lives better or worse?

On the one hand, adverts help us. They give us information about lots of things that we might not know about. They give us choices so that we know what's available and can make decisions about what to spend our money on. Another good thing is that they can amuse and entertain us. Some advertisers create wonderful ads with storylines and music. In fact, it's sometimes difficult to see what is being advertised!

However, advertisements often put pressure on us to buy things that we don't need and can't afford. We are tempted to buy more and more to be like our friends, and that's not a good thing. This can lead people into debt.

All in all, I think that advertising affects our lives badly. There are more important things in life than material things.

2 Article

A great thing about living in my area used to be the park opposite my house. There was a small lake and wide areas of grass with lots of trees. I used to spend a lot of time there with my friends. Well, not now! Last year they built two blocks of flats on the park.

I know it's important to build houses but it's such a shame to build them on park land. Local people need a place to walk and get fresh air. There are a lot of older people in this area and they used to love sitting in the park or walking their dogs there.

In addition to this, the new flats have made the road a lot busier. Often the car park for the flats is full and the people park all along the road. Sometimes people park right in front of our garage and we can't get our car out!

I'm very upset about this change in my area. Councils and builders should think much harder about where to build new homes. There aren't many parks in towns and we need to keep them.

3 Email

Hi Mark,

Great to hear from you! It sounds an interesting project. As you know, I love sport so I'm definitely the person to ask!

Regarding traditional sports, we've always loved rugby in my country. Lots of children learn it in school and we're successful in international championships too. It's an exciting game to watch and all round the country crowds of people go to watch live rugby at the weekend. Cricket is also a national sport and we're world champions at the moment! It's a popular spectator sport too and there's always a local match to go to. You can watch both these sports on TV every weekend and sometimes during the week too.

Sailing and surfing are also very popular around the coast. Unfortunately we don't see as much of these on TV as cricket and rugby, unless it's a big competition.

If I were you, I'd check out a website called SportsAustralia.com. There's a lot of information about how these sports developed in my country. The history is really interesting.

I hope this helps and good luck with the project!

Nathan

4 Story

No one had seen Andy for three days and I was starting to get worried. He wasn't answering his phone or replying to emails. I decided to go to his house and see if he was all right.

I went round after school and immediately noticed that there were no cars in the drive. His mum was always home from work by 4 o'clock. I knocked at the door but there was no reply, so I went round to the back door.

'Andy!' I called. 'Are you OK?' But no one answered. All the curtains were pulled at the windows and the house seemed empty. Then I saw something on the path. It was a phone. I picked it up – it was Andy's.

Now I was really worried. I put the phone in my pocket and started to walk home. Perhaps my dad would know what to do next. I was walking past the newsagent's when I saw the local newspaper. There was a big headline on the front page. It said, 'Do you know this man?' Underneath there was a photograph. I couldn't believe it. It was Andy's father.

SCHOLASTIC LTD.

Euston House

24 Eversholt Street

London

NW1 1DB

Publisher: Jacquie Bloese

Senior Development Editor: Sarah Silver

Editor: Fiona Davis

Designer: Dawn Wilson

Cover design: Nicolle Thomas

Photo research: Pupak Navabpour

Photo credits:

Cover M. Van Caspel/iStockphoto

Unit 1 Slkoceva, Z. Zeremski, Geber 86, C. Spencer, M. Van Caspel, Purdue9394, J. Bryson, T. Dickson/ iStockphoto; J. Kravitz, D. Ramos, J. Guerrero, L. Venance/Getty Images; Photodisc. **Unit 2** Warner Bros/Allstar; 20th Century Fox, Warner Bros/Photoshot; J. Wiberg, M. Van Caspel/iStockphoto; B. Kane, B. Jenkin/Alamy; K. VanWeel/Getty Images. **Unit 3** Maiteali, Fotografia Basica, M. Van Caspel, 4x6, I. Habur, funstock, Bonnin Studio/iStockphoto; Muscle Milk. **Unit 4** L. Norris, H. How, A. Bello/Getty Images; Albany Pictures, N. McComber, mapodile, klenger, M. Van Caspel, SbytovaMN, M. Spurny, killerb10, Judah Art/iStockphoto; Fancy Collection/Superstock. **Unit 5** Nikada, hitman photo, dem10, M. Van Caspel, Wavebreak, Maestro Books/ iStockphoto; B. Alino/AFP/Getty Images. **Unit 6** Keystone, S. Curry/AFP, C. Polk/Getty Images; K. Wothe/Alamy; william87, M. Van Caspel, derno, S. Ferdon, K. Bialasiewicz/iStockphoto. **Unit 7** Frankyleekf, Tomwang112, delectus, J. Snyder, M. Van Caspel, SbytovaMN, north light image, ntmw/iStockphoto; M. Coyne/Getty Images; R. Wareham, CulturaCreative/Alamy. **Unit 8** ItarTass/Alamy; one inch punch, M. Van Caspel, sdominick, S. Chiang, A. Ellerhorst, zhangguifu, J. Doly/iStockphoto; Beyonce/Instagram; J. Sullivan/Getty Images. **Unit 9** S. Podgorsek, cyano66, fcscafeine, T. Bridson, Sensor Spot, M. Van Caspel, william87, ranplett, M. Tamaccio, william87/iStockphoto. **Unit 10** R. Kaufman/Getty Images; South_agency, J. Doly, M. Van Caspel, Highwaystarz-Photography, pagadesign, Knight/iStockphoto; E. Miller. **Unit 11** S. Solntsev /Getty Images; mapodile, L. Medina, M. Van Caspel, A. Belomlinsky, da-kuk, vladans, A. Rosenberg, hjalmeida, L. Patrizi/ iStockphoto. **Unit 12** Sturti, M. Van Caspel, 2happy/iStockphoto; Shoosh/Alamy.

Cartoons (pages 31, 39 and 47) by Gray Jolliffe/Illustration Ltd

The publishers would like to acknowledge the following source materials:

Unit 1 'Extreme Goal Makeover' from Scholastic Choices Magazine, September 2013 **Unit 4** 'Pushing Pause' from Scholastic Choices Magazine, April 2014 'Keep Your Cool Under Pressure' from Scholastic Choices Magazine, March 2014 **Unit 6** 'The Future of Football' from Scholastic Science World Magazine, February 2015

Printed in Italy